Endorsements

⚜

The learnings of a successful life and nature all in one! I recommend this book to the recent graduate as well as someone navigating a career in today's complex organization. The insights are invaluable.

Steve Percy
Retired Chief Executive Officer
BP America

⚜

In the transition and adjustment to a new culture, the world of work, there is a total lack of understanding of how it works, why it works, and what the novice must do to succeed.

I have witnessed the internal struggle among young people and, because there is no exact equation or formula, a great deal of energy and enthusiasm is wasted and success is delayed and often time never realized.

William Boswell . . . has provided a compelling and simple analysis of the dilemma one confronts in the current environment . . . by comparing it to the behavior of animals, [he] suggests a series of solutions which are basic, elemental, and when practiced, will "boost one's career" and bring about a dynamic understanding of the values inherent therein.

Robert P. Madison, FAIA
Chairman and Chief Executive Officer
Robert P. Madison International
Architects - Engineers - Planners

Bill Boswell, known as a quiet, consummate professional, speaks volumes in *Success by Instinct*. In his professional manner he shares his wisdom and lessons on how to succeed in the world of business, be it a large organization such as a Fortune 500 company, world class nonprofit institution, or large-scale governmental operation. I highly recommend this primer as a must read on how to enhance your career by mastering and utilizing practical time-tested tools.

David W. Whitehead
Corporate Vice President
First Energy Corporation

Bill Boswell has written a unique book that is at once a useful and practical guide to personal success and a fun read. Appropriately titled *Success by Instinct*, Boswell draws on insights drawn from the natural behavior of animals, his own personal experience as one of the first African American executives to reach the top of a major corporation, and pithy sayings from writers over the ages.

His fourteen principles are not unique. The first one "know yourself," is widely written about. What is unique is how Boswell brings this point home, and makes it interesting, by describing some surprising behavior of elephants, and relating how he overcame his own early fear of public speaking.

Boswell's book will be of special interested for young people leaving school and entering the business world, or for people in mid-career thinking about where they go next.

Charles O. Rossotti
Senior Advisor, The Carlyle Group
Former Commissioner of the Internal Revenue Service

꧁

William Boswell presents a new, exciting perspective that can be embraced by anyone seeking practical advice when considering career options, encountering challenges within an organization, making decisions as business or organization leaders, or seeking personal reassurance. There are many books about the challenges of leadership, but the identification and practical use of our connections with the basic instincts of fourteen animals gives this book universal appeal and makes it a must read for life long learning.

Andrew A. Venable, J., Director
Cleveland Public Library

꧁

Refreshingly free of theories and platitudes, *Success by Instinct* provides a concrete, incisive guide for career success. This handbook is as useful for undergraduates and professional level students as it is for university career counselors and others involved in higher education. I recommend it highly as an important complement to academic pursuits.

Dr. Angela O. Terry
Former Vice Chancellor for Student Affairs
North Carolina Central University

✼

Bill Boswell's message is based upon his life's experiences and encourages you to take control of the playbook in your life and career. Simple messages are often the best messages. This book is a treasure trove of practical insights about the use of basic instinctive skills.

A correlation with the animal world is unique because the animal kingdom is without doubt one of the most structurally organized groups on the planet.

Like a good mentor, this book communicates concisely about fourteen principals. This insight into career management can serve as a well-designed road map in the current, dramatically changing organizational environment."

Theodore (Ted) Long, Jr.
Retired Partner
Ernst & Young

Success by Instinct

Success by Instinct

Use What Animals Already Know to Boost Your Career

William E. Boswell

Success by Instinct

Manufactured in the United States of America.

For information, please contact:
Brown Books Publishing Group
16200 North Dallas Parkway, Suite 170
Dallas, Texas 75248
www.brownbooks.com
972-381-0009
A New Era in Publishing™

Hardback ISBN: 1-933285-42-7
LCCN 2006924645
1 2 3 4 5 6 7 8 9 10

www.successbyinstinct.com

Dedication

This book is dedicated to my wife, Gracie, the extraordinary lady who has been my support, my confidant, and my inspiration throughout this journey.

Table of Contents

Foreword

William Boswell has uniquely organized thirty-five years of personal experiences, successes, challenges and spiritual values into an instructional narrative.

As his pastor and friend, I know firsthand William Boswell's spiritual devotion. His family commitment, professional expertise, and community service are models of leadership and excellence.

His demonstrated ability to use professionalism, the wisdom of the ages, and the lifestyles of animals to learn and teach enduring lessons is commendable. These practical and motivational examples and applications are beautiful and powerful.

I highly recommend this book for home, business, church, community, and leadership development and mentoring.

As a retired senior executive in a fortune 500 company and in a powerful government agency (the IRS), Boswell has given us a significant instrument that is user-friendly for and relevant to nearly everyone. Read it and grow.

—The Reverend Dr. Otis Moss, Jr., pastor
Olivet Institutional Baptist Church—Cleveland, Ohio
Former chair, Morehouse College board of trustees

Acknowledgements

Success by Instinct is an outgrowth of many years of organizational experience, personal knowledge, and keen observations. Even though the book's content is based primarily on things I've learned over the years, there were many individuals who assisted in translating my personal experiences into a final product.

I'd like to thank my network of invaluable contributors: Anthony, Gracie, Joseph, and Mark Boswell, William Bennett, Angela and Howard Bush, Kirstin and Paul Ford, Walter Jackson, and Andrew Venable, Jr.

You were more than generous and found time in your busy schedules to review the manuscript.

You provided gentle but candid criticism, provocative challenges, and insightful editorial comments for the manuscript.

You provided valuable insight into the development of the book's title, content, and layout.

You and other colleagues and friends provided encouragement, inspiration, enthusiasm, and moral support.

Thank you to the Cleveland Public Library for your research and to Myra Bryan for the artwork. Both the information and the illustrations were invaluable in bringing life to the chapters.

I'd also like to thank Theodore Long, Robert Madison, Steve Percy, Charles Rossotti, Hilton Smith, Angela Terry, Andrew Venable, Jr., and David Whitehead for your kind words of endorsement. Your review and valuable insights were instrumental in focusing the manuscript.

To Dr. Otis Moss, Jr., thank you for your personal review and Foreword. The thoughtful words expressed regarding my personal life, professional career, and book content are greatly appreciated.

Thanks also to the team at Brown Books Publishing Group for turning my idea into a reality:

To my publisher Milli Brown for believing in my message and its import.

To my editors Kathryn Grant, Scott Henry, and Lauren Castelli for watching my words, guarding my grammar, and policing my punctuation.

To my designer Ted Ruybal for creating a beautiful book of which I can be proud.

Finally, thank you to my family for allowing me to borrow your time for this project.

Success is built on an initial idea, a significant amount of hard work, and tremendous support from a network of committed individuals. Because of this network and their tremendous contributions, *Success by Instinct* is now a reality. I offer my sincere thanks for your invaluable input, your continuous enthusiasm, and your commitment to making this project a success.

Introduction

A moment's insight is sometimes worth a life's experience.

—Oliver Wendell Holmes (1841–1935), US jurist

We live in a highly technical environment, coexisting with many different species of animals, birds, and insects. Technology continues to change our way of life while that of these creatures has remained relatively static over the years. Because of their natural instincts, they know how to succeed in their environments. They maintain order, prosper, and create a structured environment that, upon close examination, provides many lessons we should learn and use to boost our careers in professional organizations.

Throughout my career, some of my colleagues in other professional organizations have shared many personal experiences they have encountered. As we talked, we discovered that the names changed, the cultures diverged, the employees differed, and the timing varied, but our experiences and lessons learned were very similar. We also discovered that we were all ill-equipped to face many of these issues without considerable effort. Yes, we were all well educated, articulate, and ambitious. We represented those deemed most likely to succeed after college. However, the issues we faced were not related to ability or the willingness to adapt. Instead, we noted that there were substantial differences in the requirements for advancement in professional organizations from what we had experienced. This book provides many of the lessons learned from animal instincts, from personal experiences, and from my colleagues that would have enabled us to better transition and progress in the organizational environment had we known them earlier.

Although there are many differences, there are some areas where learning in academic and professional organizations has similarities. In both, we are students learning, adjusting to the changing environment, and preparing for advancement. However, once in a professional organization, there are many other factors that become much more significant for success than in the academic environment. Attitudes, relationships, teamwork, and communication are used to evaluate potential for advancement more frequently in professional organizations than in academia. This book provides many of the major lessons, some learned from animal instincts, that are needed to transition and succeed in the professional organizational environment.

In addition, in professional organizations, our actions must be directed toward showing others the following:

- How we want to be treated

- The level of our commitment to the organization and its mission

- The values we hold and the dedication to goals

- Our eagerness to perform and excel

This book discusses these values and many other essential lessons needed in a professional organization that are not frequently or openly discussed. However, success or failure is often tied directly to the degree to which the student role is perfected, to the lessons learned, and to the application of these lessons.

This book is being presented as a practical guide based on anecdotal experience and not as a scientific research textbook. It is designed to present pertinent information and lessons to prepare readers to be responsive to the universal tests they will encounter in these organizations.

❖ The fourteen basic principles are extremely important and establish the framework on which the chapters are developed. These principles can be universally applied in most professional organizations and often in one's personal life.

❖ The major principles are all universal, practical, and uniformly accepted in professional organizations. Likewise, insects, birds, reptiles, and other animals practice these same principles successfully in their environments. Similarities between humans and these creatures are discussed to demonstrate the universality of the principles and their importance for success in every environment.

❖ The information provided throughout this book can be used as building blocks for success because it is practical and has been proven effective over many years. However, the points are more valuable today than at any other time in the past because of the increased competition for significantly fewer opportunities.

❖ The basic information is supplemented by some of my personal experiences. Although all of the situations are real, names have been changed to prevent identification. The lessons that I learned from these experiences are a result of many years of performing and observing processes in different professional organizations. These experiences are also used to reinforce the principles and other points discussed throughout the book. These lessons, if practiced, will be instrumental in preparing you for issues that you will encounter in today's professional organizations.

❖ For many of the topics discussed, relevant quotes from others have been included to provide additional insight. They represent centuries of thoughts, expressions, and a broad spectrum of reflections from the following:

- Politicians to sports icons
- World leaders to social activists
- Business leaders to entertainers
- Philosophers to personal friends
- Inventors to religious leaders
- Poets and authors to psychologists

The principles, practical information, quotations, personal experiences, and lessons are all used to emphasize the need for preparing for success in professional organizations. Additionally, if we observe the natural instincts of animals and learn from their behaviors, we can boost our careers tremendously.

Readers might be struck by the paucity of information on possible impediments to career success posed by such issues as racism, sexism, or ageism. Even though we should never acquiesce to these "isms," I have chosen not to focus on them in this book. Unfortunately, these issues still remain factors in the modern workplace, but they must be addressed on an organizational level. The focus of this book is on what we can do on a personal level to ensure our success.

It is my hope that this book will provide those seeking careers in professional organizations the necessary information on requirements, expectations, and strategies for success. If practiced, these tips will ease the transition to organizations and enable you to have a more rewarding career.

Life can only be understood backwards; but it must be lived forwards.

—Soren Kierkegaard (1813–1855), Danish philosopher

Chapter One

Self-Awareness and Elephants

There is something in every one of you that
waits and listens for the sound of the genuine in
yourself. It is the only true guide you will ever
have. And if you cannot hear it, you will all of
your life spend your days on the end of strings
that somebody else pulls.

—Howard Thurman (1900–1981), religious leader and scholar

PRINCIPLE ONE
Know Yourself, Accept Yourself, and Be Yourself Regardless of the Consequences.

The Self-Awareness of African Elephants

African elephants are colossal animals that weigh between twelve and eighteen tons, have awesome strength, and can travel at speeds of up to thirty miles per hour. With their size, strength, and speed, they could dominate the wild if they utilized these attributes for that purpose. Instead, they lead relatively gentle lives characterized by cooperation, even though they live in an environment filled with conflict. Yes, they use their dominant attributes for self-defense, but rarely in an aggressive manner. These animals have tremendous self-awareness:

- They recognize and accept their physical attributes and potential for dominance but avoid using them for that purpose.

- They are aware of their environment but do not adopt the prevalent "predator instincts."

- They understand the need for family structure for survival, so they develop and nurture this structure.

These traits indicate a level of self-awareness and a willingness to accept themselves and their lifestyle regardless of the environment.

Lesson Inspired by Nature
Understand who you are, accept your strengths and weaknesses, avoid being driven by others' expectations, and ignore negative influences in your environment. If you follow these basic guidelines, you have crossed a major threshold in your self-awareness.

Understanding Self

We are all individuals, created in nature, with some inherent good and some areas that need additional development. We must accept this as being part of our individual makeup. In spite of what may appear to be human similarities such as appearance, personality, style, and conduct, we are all unique. Because of our uniqueness, it is imperative that we work to know, be comfortable with, and develop ourselves completely. To accomplish this, we must engage in personal introspection to discover our individual qualities, determine our personal shortcomings, and plan our life's course. Of course, we do not all have the same intellect, professional interest, or personal needs. There are many personal and aspirational differences resulting from our uniqueness that are instrumental in determining our career choices. The self-awareness phase is about looking within, searching for and identifying the personal strengths and weaknesses, then choosing a career that is consistent with the individual identified.

Jim's Changing Persona

Jim, a colleague of mine, made an attempt to change his persona after many years in the organization. As an analyst, he was a hardworking, aggressive, very capable, and congenial individual. He was a tremendous team player and well respected by his colleagues and managers. Once promoted into a supervisory position, Jim's entire demeanor changed, and the tyrant in him began to emerge. He became extremely obnoxious with colleagues and disrespectful to his employees. It was difficult to understand the rationale for the dramatic change. Perhaps it was an attempt to hide insecurities, a reaction to being in an uncomfortable position, or a false perception of what the job required. Regardless of the reason, Jim changed from being a well-respected analyst to a disrespected supervisor. Eventually, after continuous counseling, failing to engender support from staff, alienating colleagues, and losing support from senior officials, Jim was asked to leave the organization. I often wondered how successful this very capable analyst would have been had he maintained his original persona as he progressed in the organization. The last I heard, Jim, with so much potential, had changed organizations several times and was again seeking employment.

Lesson: Actions for Introspection

Understand yourself and always be genuine regardless of the circumstance, position, or the environment. In doing so, your unique qualities will be obvious, and your potential for success will be greatly enhanced.

While complete self-awareness is perhaps a lofty ambition, recognize that since it is almost impossible to attain, continuous development and self-knowledge should be the goals. Regardless of where we fall within the self-awareness continuum, it is important to first engage in a significant amount of introspection before planning a lifetime career. Although introspection cannot be clearly divided into separate and distinct phases, there are numerous factors that must be included in the process. They are (1) recognition, (2) acceptance, (3) understanding strengths, (4) recognizing weaknesses, (5) identifying motivational factors, (6) determining sustaining forces, (7) preparation, (8) seeking fulfillment, and (9) recognizing others' contributions.

The most difficult thing in life is to know yourself.

—Thales (624–547 BC),
Greek philosopher, scientist, and mathematician

❖ **Recognition**—Recognition is one of the first requirements for self-awareness. It involves identifying unique personal qualities, traits, and characteristics. It also involves determining or identifying our individual skill sets, our ambitions, our motivations, our directions, and all of the factors that are important to us as individuals. During the recognition phase, we must be brutally honest and realistic and avoid entertaining nonsensical expectations. We must recognize that our individual contribution may not be as the next astronaut, the next great scientist, the next great musician, or even the next great sports legend. However, we may be the individual who leaves a legacy in education, politics, or even organizational advancement. The important thing to realize is that we all have unique individual talents that, once developed, could be instrumental in leading us to rewarding careers. Self-awareness should not result in a personal indictment, a minimization of our skills, or a criticism of our abilities. Instead, it should serve as the realization that our skills and career choices should be in harmony. If we fail in the recognition process, we hinder growth, delay development, and fail to reach our potential.

> **If I didn't define myself for myself, I would be crunched into other people's fantasies for me and eaten alive.**
>
> —Audre Lorde (1934–1992), US writer, activist, and educator

❖ **Acceptance**—Self-acceptance means to be comfortable and at peace with one's personal qualities, ambitions, motivations, and other identified characteristics. It is also in acceptance that we recognize that we all have tremendous strengths and many areas in need of development. These are the qualities that reflect individual differences. Remember how elephants recognize and accept their position in their environment? At the acceptance stage, it is not necessary to broadcast strengths or advertise weaknesses. Instead, we need to quietly recognize and understand them for ourselves. As we recognize, respect, and accept these personal qualities, we become aware of our possibilities and our limitations. This is not suggesting that we put unnecessary expectations or limitations on ourselves; instead, we must accept and develop our personal skills to their maximum potential.

Self-awareness does not involve considering what friends, family, or others may have done. We should not try to duplicate the process they used, the paths they followed, or even the successes or failures they may have encountered. We should never allow our identity to be defined by others regardless of the following:

- How influential or successful they may be

- The expectations they have for us

- The pressure they exert over us

- The investment they are willing to make or have made on our behalf

Of course, we must always be willing to accept input and listen to advice from others. However, we must focus on accepting and building on our personal qualities. Until we accept this reality, it will be difficult to identify, focus, and establish realistic expectations for ourselves. It is difficult to succeed in life just being ourselves, and it is almost impossible if we fail to be genuine, forthright, and accept our individuality. If we cannot accept ourselves, surely we cannot be true to others.

This lack of forthrightness in self-acceptance makes the attainment of our goals much more difficult. This phase refers to accepting the individual we identified in the self-awareness process.

The Star Athlete Dream

I vividly recall, as a youngster, dreaming of becoming a star athlete. However, my lack of athletic ability was the sobering fact that forced me to recognize that being a professional athlete was a tremendous dream, but it was an unrealistic expectation. Recognizing and accepting this reality was necessary before I moved forward. Although it was perfectly normal to dream, once the impossibility of the dream was evident, it was then time to wake up, focus, and get real.

> ## Lesson: Dreams or Reality
> Dream if you must, but recognize and accept your personal strengths and weaknesses. Build on the strengths that are essential to reach your goals and strive to improve your weaknesses. This combination will enhance your potential for success.

Recognizing and Accepting Fear

Self-awareness, the necessity for recognition, and acceptance of individuality all have very strong personal meaning for me. Throughout much of my early life, I had a tremendous fear of speaking in large group environments. Of course, some of this fear related to confidence. Perhaps the major factor was an underlying belief that my background, education, and experiences were inadequate to make meaningful input. This belief left me thinking that my contribution or input to discussions would be shallow and that others would observe my lack of preparedness. It was also apparent to me that I could not reach my goal as long as this weakness plagued me. Yes, I recognized, understood, and accepted the rationale for the fear:

- An early education beginning in a one-room, segregated school

- A childhood on a farm in a small rural community with little external exposure

- A childhood with a loving family but with meager resources for survival

Although recognition and acceptance were necessary, those alone were not enough to move me toward my goal. The most significant factor was to establish a personal improvement plan that would address the problem and remove this fear. I chose to force myself into situations that required me to engage in public speaking. My initial step was joining and attending weekly lunchtime meetings of Toastmasters International, an organization dedicated to helping individuals build more effective communication skills. After several years of Toastmasters, I enrolled in and completed several Dale Carnegie courses, designed to improve my extemporaneous and public speaking skills. The final step of my immersion plan was to teach evenings and weekends at the local community college. The teaching continued for a number of years until my level of comfort with group discussions, extemporaneous speaking, and public speaking had improved tremendously. While recognition and acceptance of my weakness were critical steps, planning a course of action and dedicating and committing myself to a plausible solution were imperative.

Lesson on Actions for Improvement

Recognizing and accepting your personal weaknesses is necessary; however, developing a program to remove them is just as essential. Your success is dependent upon your sincerity, dedication, and willingness to invest in workable solutions.

❖ **Understanding Strengths**—All of us have tremendous strengths, and it is important that we recognize and understand these individual strengths. The strengths referred to here are not physical, but they are the traits, skills, characteristics, and qualities that distinguish us from others. They are the attributes needed to sustain us throughout our careers. They are our individual assets and are often distinctly different from those of our families or friends. Understanding strengths is essential, and the knowledge gained will allow us to direct our efforts toward producing meaningful results. In order to reach our long-term goal, we may need to continually develop our strengths to maximize potential. We must develop our individual strengths to the highest level and channel them in a meaningful, productive, and appropriate direction. It is only through identifying, developing, and channeling our strengths that we prepare ourselves for the positive recognition we are seeking and rightfully deserve.

Somehow we learn who we really are and then live with that decision.

—Eleanor Roosevelt (1884–1962),
US columnist, lecturer, and wife of US president

❖ **Recognizing Weaknesses**—Regardless of the success an individual achieves in life, everyone has some areas that need improvement. Recognizing our personal shortcomings is not for indictment purposes. Instead, knowing they exist, understanding what triggers them, and accepting these realities are the major steps in the self-awareness phase. There are often well-meaning family members, friends, or acquaintances who are always eager to point out weaknesses and offer advice on how best to improve them. I am not suggesting that we ignore advice from others. Recognize that even though they may have our best interests at heart, their advice may not be reasonable since it may not be appropriate for our individual circumstances. Advice givers do not have a thorough knowledge of our hopes, dreams, and aspirations. Instead, this is the knowledge or the personal self-awareness that the recognition step provides. Notice here that I am not suggesting that we accept our assessment or even the assessments of others and be content just knowing we have weaknesses. Recognition without taking action is no better than nonrecognition. What I am suggesting is that recognition is just the first step before beginning the arduous task of continuously striving to improve. It is only through improving our weaknesses that we become stronger individuals, better prepared for and closer to reaching the pinnacle of success we are seeking.

Unacceptable Advice

The need for a personal assessment and action plan was reinforced when an acquaintance and coworker of mine offered some fatherly advice. Because of his many years in the organization, significant business experience, and my inexperience, I was eager to hear his advice. At that time, I had recently joined the organization, formulated my professional goal, and was seeking advice and counsel wherever possible. His advice was: "If you ever want to be successful in this organization, you will need to change your personality. You must be more assertive, loud, and flamboyant to get people's attention." While I thoroughly agree that assertiveness is essential, in effect he was advising me to make drastic changes to my personality to reflect that assertiveness. Out of respect for the individual, I accepted his comments and indicated that I would carefully consider that advice. However, I was not ready or willing to accept his advice. As a young man, I was always relatively reserved and perhaps, in some ways, acted somewhat more maturely than my years. I told him later, "I will continue to be assertive, I will continue to refine my skills, I will refocus my effort toward more networking, I will continue to focus on professionalism, and I will ensure that my goals are realistic, but I am not willing to change my personality." I was not prepared to change who I was just to attain success in any organization. I could not envision spending my entire career living a fictitious life that would have been difficult or impossible to maintain. Even if it were possible, it would have been an extremely uncomfortable existence.

Lesson: Advice vs. Honesty

Always be willing to listen to advice and counsel from others, but remember to temper that advice if it prevents you from being honest and forthright. It is more important to be yourself than to blindly follow another person's prescription for success.

❖ **Identifying Motivational Factors**—Sometimes we may share similar strengths and weaknesses, yet we are motivated by different factors or circumstances. Surely, African elephants' motivation is not to dominate their environment. Instead, they are motivated by other factors. Factors that motivate some of us may have no impact on others. As part of self-awareness, we should identify or recognize the factors that motivate us and provide that little extra push to continue advancing in the competitive environment. There are many factors that motivate individuals, including, but not limited to, the following:

- **Prestige**—The desire for external adulation or admiration from others

- **Challenge**—The exhilaration from having to overcome a major obstacle

- **Power**—The quest for supremacy or the desire to exert influence over others

- **Self-Satisfaction**—The internal drive for personal accomplishment or success

- **Fear**—The concern for the consequences of failure that outweighs the drive for success

- **Competition**—The adrenaline rush that results from competing with others rather than from victory or success

- **Material Possessions**—The desire to accumulate wealth

- **Integrity**—The quest to be honest and to avoid the appearance of impropriety

The purpose of this phase in self-awareness is to understand our personal motivational factors. It is not to pass judgment on their significance or to determine whether they are appropriately aligned. Once we identify our own motivational factors, we have gained important personal insight, are better prepared, and can utilize this knowledge to position ourselves for eventual success.

Personal Motivation

The factors that motivated me were the desire to be personally satisfied with my performance, the challenge of overcoming obstacles, and the maintenance of my personal integrity. There is a saying that I consistently followed: "Every day you have to look into the mirror, and you must like that person who is looking back." Throughout my career, my motivation was to be personally satisfied with that person looking back at me. My satisfaction test was perhaps more severe than others'. However, I was confident that if I satisfied myself, others would no doubt be impressed. Yes, recognition was important, but not for personal gratification. It was important because it indicated awareness, acceptance, a step toward continued advancement, and the eventual achievement of my personal goals.

Lesson on Motivation

Identify the factors that motivate you. Accept them, build on them, and avoid being sidetracked by unimportant issues.

❖ **Determining Sustaining Forces**—Our sustaining force is the energy that supports us during difficult periods. Yes, as we pursue our goals, there will be many very positive experiences. However, in spite of our effort to avoid impediments, there will be some very difficult days and situations that we must overcome to achieve success. To prepare for these inevitable occurrences, we should identify the factors that sustain us, give us comfort, provide strength, and give us the impetus to continue our forward progress. The identification, understanding, and nurturing of these forces will enable us to maintain a positive attitude, avoid disenchantment, and maintain focus during the difficult periods.

Knowing others is wisdom, knowing yourself is enlightenment.

—Lao Tzu (sixth century BC), Chinese philosopher

❖ **Preparation**—During the practice of self-awareness, it is important to recognize that we will engage in many successful experiences and encounter many agonizing failures. Although both success and failure are inevitable, accepting this inevitability is essential for success. Adequate personal and professional development will prepare us mentally, physically, and intellectually and serve as a confidence builder. This preparation will enable us to maintain focus and provide the assurance for success. Accepting success while maintaining humility and using accomplishments as building blocks is essential. However, for most of us, accepting failure as a building block to character is a significantly larger challenge. Being prepared to accept success or overcome hurdles as they occur is essential. Confronting adversity can be devastating if unprepared.

> **Ask yourself: Am I doing the things that make me happy? Are my thoughts of noble character? How can I simplify my life? What are my talents? Does my work satisfy my soul? Am I giving value to my existence? How can I improve my way of life?**
>
> —Alfred A. Montapert, US motivational author

❖ **Seeking Fulfillment**—It is extremely important that during the practice of self-awareness we identify and understand the things that will provide a level of fulfillment in life. Elephants appear to nurture their family structure as a means of fulfillment. Even though fulfillment is a personal issue that is uniquely different for each individual, it clearly impacts the level of happiness we experience in our lives. Since we spend a considerable amount of our lives preparing for, focusing on, or working toward our career goals, it is imperative that we enjoy, be content with, and be satisfied with our careers. If we also seek and incorporate other elements that provide fulfillment and a level of joy to our lives, we are likely to do the following:

- Devote more time and effort to accomplishing our goals

- Expend less energy

- Make more significant contributions

- Receive greater rewards

- Improve the quality of our lives immensely

Likewise, without fulfillment, we lose focus, drive, and energy. As a result, small tasks become extremely laborious.

Personal Fulfillment

Fulfillment has always been a high priority in my life and was brought into focus with an article that appeared in a local newspaper announcing my promotion to vice president in my organization. The business section's headline, in big bold print, was "The Most Influential Man You've Never Heard Of." Although the article was extremely positive, some of my friends and colleagues viewed the headline as negative. However, I was comfortable with the heading, very pleased with the article, and even considered the headline a personal accomplishment. The reason for my sense of accomplishment was that I had achieved success without seeking external exposure throughout my career. My goal was to gain recognition, maintain an extremely high internal organizational profile, minimize external public exposure, and maintain personal privacy to enjoy with family and friends. Since I have always been a relatively private person, this privacy was extremely important to me. Privacy meant recognizing and accepting that professional life must offer a place for personal comfort. My ambition was also to stay involved with community service projects to assist mankind. Although my professional goal was to become a senior executive in a Fortune 50 organization, I also had personal and societal goals. For me, success entailed a meaningful and extremely successful career, a public life devoted to serving humanity, and an enjoyable personal life. This is not to suggest that my approach was a recipe for success or that everyone should follow this same script. What I am suggesting, however, is that professional achievement, community service, and family enjoyment were the factors that provided fulfillment in my personal life.

> # Lesson on Personal Fulfillment
> While it is important to recognize, accept, and do the things that will promote your professional career, it is just as important to seek personal fulfillment. The combination of career success and personal fulfillment will improve your life satisfaction.

❖ **Recognizing Others' Contributions**—Recognize that the path we choose has been partially prepared by many others. Regardless of the height of our climb or the depth of our despair, understand that success is not totally a result of our efforts. There were many individuals who preceded us, performed admirably under very difficult circumstances, and laid much of the foundation upon which we stand. We may be aware of the roles some of the individuals played; however, we may be unaware of many unsung heroes and heroines who have significantly contributed to our success. Regardless of our personal knowledge, we must continue to build on these legacies or foundations such that we too can leave a legacy for future generations. Knowing, understanding, and accepting this reality enables us to continue striving for success and driving toward our long-term goals.

Developing a much-needed understanding of ourselves, our strengths, our weaknesses, our motivational factors, and our sustaining forces is clearly a necessity for every individual. Self-knowledge, self-acceptance, self-improvement, and self-fulfillment are all paramount and essential as we embark on the journey toward fulfilling our goals. What I am suggesting is no different from what we see in nature. Remember African elephants? They practice activities such as recognition, awareness, and acceptance in their environment. It appears that self-awareness is universal and shared by both humans and animals. For us, it is necessary to promote well-being, gain self-fulfillment, and accomplish personal goals.

The greatest thing in the world is to know how to be one's self.

—Michel Eyquem de Montaigne (1533–1592), French essayist

Chapter Two

Adaptability and Chameleons

Unless you try to do something beyond what you
have already mastered, you will never grow.

—Ronald E. Osborn, writer and author

PRINCIPLE TWO
Acknowledge That Adaptability Is Essential to an Effective Transition.

Adaptable Chameleons

Chameleons are relatively small reptiles that use their natural color to hide or blend into their surroundings. They must blend because they are too slow to pursue insects, their food source, or to escape their predators. They are unique in that they have the ability to look in two directions simultaneously, see in color, and change their exterior colors and patterns almost instantaneously. There is a misconception, however, that chameleons arbitrarily and frequently change their colors without purpose, just as we change outfits. Instead, they change for specific reasons:

- To blend into their environment when the world around them changes

- To adjust to air, temperature, or light changes

- To communicate with other chameleons

- When startled by predators

It is chameleons' ability to change their colors for specific purposes and fend for themselves immediately after birth that enables their survival.

> ## Lesson Inspired by Nature
>
> To accomplish your goals, achieve success, and advance in professional organizations, you must be as adaptable as chameleons. It is essential that you understand when change is required, know how to blend into the organizational environment, and be able to thrive instantaneously.

Reaching new goals sometimes means letting go of past relationships and situations.

—Dorothy Wagner, PhD, US psychotherapist

Effective Transitioning Requires Change

There is a strong belief by many that performance in an academic environment is the primary measure of how well we will perform in professional organizations. While there is definitely a relationship, success in one does not readily translate into success in the other. There are significant differences in the qualities needed for success in the two environments. After years of formal training, we become very proficient in the academic approach. The approach is to learn the assigned lesson from a textbook, take a test, perform well, and be rewarded with a degree. In professional organizations, there is a paradigm shift, and the process is completely reversed. The test is taken first, the lesson revealed, and the acknowledgement of success or advancement is dependent upon how well the implicit lessons are learned. Unfortunately, the tests are random, unscheduled, and there are no textbooks or other reference materials from which to prepare. Because of the significant differences, the transition from the academic environment into professional organizations must be approached with the recognition, knowledge, and understanding that our energy and actions must be refocused if we are to be successful. In effect, we must be just as effective as chameleons in adapting to our new environment.

Accept the challenges, so that you may feel the exhilaration of victory.

—George S. Patton (1885–1945), US Army general

Although the academic model is successful, we must adopt the chameleons approach, make a change, and adjust to the new environment to achieve success in professional organizations. There are eight distinct areas where the focus must be significantly different when we transition from the academic environment to professional organizations. These areas are (1) selection process, (2) expectations, (3) evaluations, (4) interpersonal relations, (5) advancement, (6) structure, (7) adaptability, and (8) personal management.

❖ **Selection Process**—In an academic environment, advancement is based almost exclusively on historical accomplishment. We are selected for college because of our past high school records, test results, extracurricular activities, and other intangibles. A personal interview is often omitted from the selection process. The selection criteria are relatively similar among schools, even though the emphasis may differ. In professional organizations, historical accomplishments are significant and the basis for opening the door. However, potential and organizational fit are the major factors that determine most selections. The emphasis shifts since there are many candidates with similar educational backgrounds and interests. The selection process is based on the expected culture fit, potential for growth, and expected contribution to the organization. Because of the change in emphasis, the interview process is a critical step in the transitioning process. Be aware that past academic achievements will not overcome a failed interview. There are numerous individuals with stellar academic credentials, but they find it extremely difficult to gain employment. Always project a positive image, be aggressive, prepare for the interview, know the organization, develop relevant questions, and promote your strengths. Understand the significance, focus energy on the selection process, and do not rely on your historical accomplishments.

❖ **Expectations**—There are significant differences between expectations in academic environments and professional organizations. In academia, we are students pursuing additional knowledge, and our professors are willing to share their knowledge. However, in professional organizations, we are expected to give. Our supervisors and coworkers will share company policies, customs, and work habits, but these are only office basics. We are expected to have the skill set, be committed, make the extra effort, ask the necessary questions, and be aggressive in the pursuit of the information we really need to succeed. We should not expect, nor will we experience, the student-teacher relationship that existed in academia. Remember, we were selected for our expected contribution to the organization rather than for our potential to gain additional knowledge. It is important that we understand this difference and govern ourselves accordingly if we are to be successful in professional organizations.

❖ **Evaluations**—There is also a significant difference in the basis for personal evaluations in academic and professional organizational environments. In academia, the focus is on the end product. We are evaluated based on the results of an examination, class participation, research projects, or maybe even an oral presentation. Seldom is our success based on subjective factors. The time and points of evaluation are fixed, and we have the opportunity to prepare ourselves. In professional organizations, the evaluations are continuous and based as much on the process as the end results. There is an ongoing evaluation of how we conduct ourselves, work with others, communicate, operate within the team, and keep management informed. While the end product is important and the completeness and professionalism will be evaluated, much of the evaluation process is completed well before the end of the project. Yes, we must focus our effort on completing a thorough and professional end product. However, we must also recognize that the personal evaluation process in professional organizations is continuous, much more involved, and includes many more subjective measures.

A man is the part he plays among his fellows. He is not isolated; he cannot be. His life is made up of the relationships he bears to other—is made or marred by those relationships, guided by them, judged by them, expressed in them.

—Woodrow Wilson (1856–1924),
US president, governor, and college president

❖ **Interpersonal Relations**—Interpersonal relations are important in every sector of society. Social skills aid in the development process and assist in producing well-rounded individuals. However, strong interpersonal skills are not necessarily the basis for advancement in academia. We could, although it is not recommended, advance in an academic environment by focusing primarily on educational achievement and ignoring the personal aspects of development. Additionally, we have the flexibility to select our associates so that we avoid personality conflicts and other distractions. We do not have this same flexibility in professional organizations. We do not have the flexibility to select group members, move to another group, isolate ourselves, or avoid personal contact and expect to be successful. We are expected to build professional relationships with members in the group. Failure to develop these relations is perceived as our inability to transition, our having poor social skills, or our having ineffective group dynamics. We must develop relationships with our team members, be professional with our competitors, avoid personality conflicts, and demonstrate strong interpersonal skills, even under adverse conditions. The ability to adjust our actions will separate us from our peers and promote the advancement of our careers.

> **No matter how much work a man can do, no matter how engaging his personality may be, he will not advance far in business if he can not work through others.**
>
> —John Craig

❖ **Advancement**—In the academic environment, advancement is relatively objective and based primarily on the completion of predetermined requirements. As we advance, we are presented with new educational challenges. Success is determined based primarily on the successful completion of the requirements. The performance of our peers does not enter into advancement decisions. There is a huge paradigm shift once we enter professional organizations. Although knowledge is important and critical for successful performance, a significant amount of emphasis is placed on other more subjective qualities. Professional organizations operate primarily through teams, and our ability to function as active members of teams is critical for advancement. Interpersonal skills, adaptability, sharing, and dependability are all critical when advancement decisions are made within professional organizations. Additionally, since the criteria for advancement are more subjective, there are no clearly defined requirements that will automatically ensure advancement. It is not limited to our personal accomplishments, but it is often based on our ability to outperform our peers. Our advancement is dependent upon recognizing these significant differences, making the necessary personal adjustments, and adapting to the environment. We must be just as effective in adjusting to our environment as chameleons are in adjusting to theirs if we are to be successful.

❖ **Structure**—There is significant structure in most academic environments since educational systems must address the needs of large groups. In addition, the cost to personalize the process would be prohibitive. The requirements for advancement, expected time to complete the requirements, and points to celebrate (i.e., graduation) are all clearly defined. There are few professional organizations where the process is structured for every individual. Every organization is unique and every career distinct. Every individual has different skill sets, aspirations, work ethics, and career paths. As a result, we must learn to operate and thrive in relatively unstructured environments. However, it is important that we create our own personal structure if we are to be successful in professional organizations. We must choose our organizations, identify our goals, develop our implementation plans, manage our careers, and pursue opportunities for advancement. It is the ability to create structure in a relatively unstructured environment that will determine our success or failure.

❖ **Adaptability**—We must be flexible and more adaptable in professional organizations than in academic settings. Most academic settings follow a uniform pattern for developing requirements. From an early age, there is an expectation that all students will be exposed to similar, basic material, and that exposure will be increased uniformly as they progress. Yes, there are academic settings where the requirements are more rigorous than others, but the process is relatively similar. However, every professional organization is different in its expectations and requirements for success:

- We must adapt to the organization's unique customs and practices as well as the many written and unwritten organizational guidelines.

- The decision-making process is primarily hierarchical. Since we operate in teams and our assignments are part of a larger project or organizational goal, decisions must be made in conjunction with others. Consultation is important since the decision could impact the outcome of a project or affect the team.

- The environment is continuously changing, expectations are often poorly defined, evaluation points and criteria are different, relationships must be developed and nurtured, and success criteria are very subjective.

- The skill is more intense. We are often confronted with a number of unstructured tasks with competing timelines. Additionally, our ability to effectively manage many tasks— our personal and professional lives, our relationships with team members, and our interaction with senior officials— makes organizational skills one of the most significant tools that we must master to be effective.

We often refer to this process of adapting to our new environment as the acculturation process. However, it is a survival skill for chameleons. The degree to which we adapt to the new environment and aggressively pursue our goals will determine the level of success we achieve in professional organizations.

A Failed Transition

During an early supervisory position, I hired Art, who was a well-trained accountant with an MBA from a prestigious university. My expectation was that his background would be valuable to my organization and his academic skills would be easily applied in a professional organizational environment. However, Art struggled from day one and failed to adjust to this environment's decision-making process, interpersonal relations, and personal management. Although in an academic environment he had succeeded on many projects and made the necessary decisions, they were all in a structured environment. In spite of repeated counseling sessions, he never quite made the adjustment and eventually left the organization. He simply wasn't as adaptable as a chameleon. The last I heard, he was working as an accountant in a small community service organization.

Lesson on Transitioning

It is important to excel in the academic environment. However, it is critical to realize that your prior success will not automatically translate into success in an organizational environment. The evaluation criteria for the two are uniquely different, and you must make the adjustment to effectively transition.

❖ **Personal Management**—Although the ability to manage ourselves is important in our personal lives and in academia, it is essential in professional organizations. There is nothing more important for success than the ability to effectively manage our personal lives and professional careers, especially in an unstructured environment. Personal management is the capacity to successfully maintain a balance of the following:

- **Time**—Devoting sufficient time to a career to be successful while maintaining balance in life

- **Preparation**—Identifying personal requirements and developing the necessary skills to succeed in organizations

- **Interpersonal Relations**—Developing the skills to work well with others, even when there is adversity

- **Work Ethic**—Staying focused and maintaining a strong, determined effort on every project assigned

- **Commitment**—Committing ourselves to the organization and to personal performance excellence regardless of the perceived importance of the assignment

- **Initiative**—Being proactive rather than reactive in identifying requirements and completing over and above the minimal requirements

- **Teamwork**—Accepting that success is dependent upon the ability to work well in a team

- **Professionalism**—Conducting ourselves in a manner that others recognize and respect, because of our skills, diplomacy, integrity, and image

- **Performance**—Maintaining a performance level that is technically strong, thorough, and professional at all times

Yes, it is essential that we are successful in managing ourselves if we are to achieve success in our careers and accomplish our goals. Managing ourselves or our "Personal Brand" is essential for success. The way we manage our "Personal Brand" determines our value (personal stock price or bumper sticker) in the organization.

We enter professional organizations after having been trained in an academic setting to think, reason, respond, and act in a certain manner. Immediately after entering the new environment, we are expected to change our focus and be proficient in an environment in which we have had little training and no significant exposure. Chameleons must survive alone immediately after birth, instantaneously make changes in their colors and patterns, and continuously adjust to their environment. It is a similar type of transition that we must make when entering professional organizations. Although there are many skills needed to advance, they will all be unimportant if we fail to make the paradigm shift and effectively adapt to the new environment.

Nature gives to every time and season some beauties of its own; and from morning to night, as from cradle to the grave, is but a succession of changes so gentle and easy that we can scarcely mark their progress.

—Charles Dickens (1812–1870), English novelist

Chapter Three

Goals and Ants

The tragedy in life doesn't lie in not reaching your goals. The tragedy lies in having no goals to reach. It isn't a calamity to die with dreams unfilled, but it is certainly a calamity not to dream. It is not a disaster to be unable to capture your ideals, but it is a disaster to have no ideals to capture.

—Benjamin Mays (1894–1984),
US religious leader, college president, educator, and activist

PRINCIPLE THREE
Establish Goals to Add Direction, Purpose, Focus, and Meaning to Life.

The Goal-Seeking Ants

Ants' actions have often been described as resembling human civilization. Their daily activities rank extremely high on the scale of intelligence. They have been described as busy, efficient, and enigmatic because of their large communities, elaborate habitation, roadways, cooperative achievement, and social organization. In spite of their apparent specialization, much of their effort is directed toward providing food for the colony. Throughout the summer, they labor long hours to accomplish their goal. Their effort is often the symbol of diligence and industry. Some of the most impressive areas for food storage have been found in dry or semi-desert lands where rainfall provides few opportunities to support a rich food supply. It has been reported that the food storage of the North American desert ant has been so extensive that colonies have survived droughts that lasted as long as ten years.

Lesson Inspired by Nature

Ants identify, organize themselves, and diligently pursue the accomplishment of their goals in spite of the environment. You should be just as diligent in identifying, pursuing, and accomplishing your personal and professional goals in spite of the circumstances encountered.

Well-Defined, Concrete, and Realistic Goals

In *Motivation and Goal-Setting,* Jim Cairo state that "goals are conceptual: they represent the ideal state to which you aspire—the ones that guide all your actions." Goals are the plan, the objective, the ambition, the aim, the destination, or that which we are determined to focus our efforts on attaining. They are the career blueprint, the guide, or the map we plan to follow to reach our career destination. Goals add purpose, focus, and meaning to life and careers. It is unacceptable to allow our careers to meander without purpose or to leave the planning in the hands of people who really have no vested interest in our success. We must plan our futures and ensure that we stay on course toward reaching our destination. We have the interest and commitment to our goals. It is unlikely we will successfully complete the journey to our destination if we fail to plan. However, if we behave like ants (i.e., establish our goals and know our direction), we can focus our total efforts toward accomplishing them. This will improve the likelihood of our success.

Establish Goals Early

Some years ago, my organization acquired another organization and I was sent to review its administrative operations. It was general knowledge that the headquarters of the acquired organization would eventually be closed. As a result, many of the employees were not motivated or enthusiastic about their career opportunities. One employee's action, I will call him Tom, could not go unnoticed since he had a roadmap spread across his desk and was busily highlighting it and writing on a notepad. Although it did not affect my review, I was curious as to how this roadmap affected Tom's daily work routine. After it continued into the second day, I finally asked Tom what he was working on, and he responded jovially. He stated that he had always wanted to take a cross-country trip to visit the Grand Canyon and Yellowstone National Park, and he was now planning that trip. The response was particularly intriguing since he was utilizing work time to plan for a vacation that, he later stated, was nearly a year away. That vacation was so important to him that he did not want it to fail. Well in advance of the journey, he identified his final destination, outlined the specific route, estimated the travel time, and highlighted the points of interest along the way. His vacation plan was realistic, specific, and written.

Over the years, I have gone through the same ritual and planned every detail of a vacation just to ensure success. Occasionally, I adjusted the route because of obstacles or detours, but my destination remained fixed. I have also followed the same routine whether traveling by airplane or just utilizing the city bus; identify the destination and plan the best method to reach that destination.

Lesson: Career Planning

To achieve success you must establish your goals early. Plan every aspect of the journey to ensure that you not only reach the destination, but enjoy the scenery along the way. If for just a few weeks of vacation you are willing to spend considerable time planning your destination, charting your route, estimating travel time, and identifying the stops along the way, then surely you should be just as diligent when planning your lifelong career.

If you don't know where you are going, how can you expect to get there?

—Basil S. Walsh, US author

When we establish our goals, they must be S.M.A.R.T.: (1) specific and concrete, (2) measurable, (3) attainable and realistic, (4) relevant to our individual interests and skills, and (5) thorough (implementation plan).

❖ **Specific and Concrete**—Goals should establish the target for which to aim, and they should be concise, clearly defined, and most importantly, very specific. Goals should identify the destination, such as "To Become a Corporate Chief Executive Officer," rather than identifying all of the sights along the journey. Goals do not attempt to identify *how* they will be accomplished. Instead, they should identify *what* will be accomplished, or the final destination. They should not be so detailed or precise as to incorporate all of the parameters or steps needed for achievement. In fact

   • we may not know precisely how goals can be achieved;

   • goals could be altered as time passes or as more information becomes available.

In spite of the potential for deviations, establishing goals is essential. Without them, we will arrive at a destination; it may not be our chosen destination or even the destination that will bring us contentment.

Once the goals have been identified, they should be written and easily accessible, and constantly used as a point of reference or reminder of the destination. Having this written document is extremely useful as we experience success in our careers. It serves as a reminder that individual accomplishments are milestones along the journey but not the final destination. Similarly, it serves as a beacon, a focal point, or a reminder to press ahead during periods when we experience failures. This written document thus becomes the guiding light throughout our careers.

You must have long-term goals to keep you from being frustrated by short-range failures.

—Charles Noble, US author

Once we identify and write down our goals, we must believe that they can be accomplished. In *Think and Grow Rich*, Napoleon Hill states that "one comes finally to believe whatever one repeats to one's self, whether the statement be true or false." He suggests that "any plan or purpose may be placed in the mind through repetition of thought." Our goals should be treated in the same manner; we must believe that they can be accomplished, and keep them ever present in our consciousness. This practice requires forming a mental image or visualizing the goals and their accomplishment. It is through the identification, documentation, repetition, and visualization of our goals that we position ourselves to be successful in our careers.

Before you begin a thing, remind yourself that difficulties and delays quite impossible to foresee are ahead. . . . You can only see one thing clearly and that is your goal. Form a mental vision of that and cling to it through thick and thin.

—Kathleen Norris, poet, author, and writer

❖ **Measurable**—The implementation plan should include parameters or points where the level of progress can be measured. For example, if the implementation plan includes the steps, or touch points, necessary to reach the destination, they can also be used as measuring points. Include the amount of time necessary to complete each step.

In effect, the steps are the mile markers we establish for our journey. Once the implementation plan has been completed following this process, it can easily be determined if we are on target. It also provides the necessary information to adjust direction, as needed, to reach the identified goal.

Measurable Steps to Reach a Goal

Immediately after completing my undergraduate degree, I accepted a sales training position with a major retail establishment. The program was designed to develop retail store managers. There were a minimum of four and a maximum of six clearly identifiable positions to master before I would be considered for the position of store manager. The expectations were defined in that each position required a minimum of six and a maximum of twelve months to master. The goal had been established: a retail store manager. The implementation plan was specific and measurable in that it provided an identifiable target, the steps required, and the time frame on which to reach the destination.

Lesson: Measurable Goals

Ensure that measurable targets are built into your implementation plan. They will enable you to maintain focus, assess progress, and adjust direction, if necessary, to accomplish your goals.

First make up your mind what you want to do . . . be . . . have. Set your goals; establish your priorities. Work out plans to reach these goals then measure life and your days accordingly.

—Alfred A. Montapert, US motivational author

❖ **Attainable and Realistic**—Goals should be realistic and attainable. They should be set high enough to stretch our abilities, talents, or skills but set at a level where they can be attained. If goals are unattainable, we set ourselves up for failure. Failure increases frustration, negatively impacts confidence, lowers self-esteem, and leads to the eventual loss of interest. If goals are established too low just to ensure success, we may reach them without much effort. However, we risk not reaching our full potential, losing direction, and possibly becoming bored once the goals are attained. Without goals, we lose meaning, purpose, and focus for our careers. Establishing realistic goals is all about reaching that happy medium such that we can maintain focus on the destination. They should be set high enough to reach our potential but fair enough to allow the possibility for success. Tough goals can be achieved. Remember how desert ants stored food and water through a long drought? Similarly, we should have stretch goals that can be attained only with considerable effort.

> ## My definition of success is achieving the goals one set for one's self whatever they may be.
>
> —Michael T. Halbouty (1909–2004), US geoscientist

❖ **Relevant to Our Individual Interests and Skills**—When identifying goals, make sure that they are consistent with our interests and skills. We are all unique individuals with different talents, strengths, weaknesses, and gifts that can be utilized in many ways. We must be aware of our specific skills and direct our goal development toward areas consistent with those interests or talents. As a result of our self-awareness, we have a more realistic view of our interests and skills. For example, if our interest is to work in a private setting, we should not choose a career in sales. By establishing our goals in areas that are consistent with our interests or skills, we (1) decrease the level of stress, (2) reduce the potential for loss of interest, (3) increase the level of enjoyment, and (4) improve the potential for success. Likewise, if we fail to recognize our skills and interests, we increase the possibility of failure.

If the established goals are consistent with our interests and we are committed to accomplishing them, we can withstand impediments that may be encountered along the journey. Often, as a result of these impediments, accomplishment may be delayed. However, a delay should not necessarily require the abandonment of our goals.

A Dream Deferred

Many of us can clearly identify our goals, develop the implementation plan, and immediately begin working toward their accomplishment. There are others that, for many reasons, must delay their dreams. My wife is one of those individuals. Her goal was, and still is, to contribute to social issues in a scholarly manner for the advancement of health issues for the elderly. Although her goal was laser clear, it was interrupted by pressing family issues and her ensuring nourishment, development, and well-being of our children. Although this delayed her necessary preparation, it did not eliminate her goal or the pursuit of her dream. When the opportunity was available, she began pursuing her goal, received her PhD, and, at the age when most of her friends were contemplating retirement, began the process of contributing in a scholarly manner to issues affecting the aged. Although she has not yet completely accomplished her goal, the critical factor is that tremendous progress has been made primarily because of her refusal to allow her dream to fade.

Lesson on Focus

Events in life may present significant challenges or require a temporary focus on other priorities. However, if you continue focusing on your goals and never allow them to fade, the impediments will not derail your success.

❖ **Thorough (Implementation Plan)**—Once the goals have been identified, we can begin outlining the steps—developing an implementation plan—to ensure achievement. If the path to our destination is defined, this step is relatively straightforward. We can then identify other parameters that we expect to encounter along the journey. However, since most of the information is rarely available, we should be as specific as possible while recognizing that additional information can be incorporated later as it becomes available.

The process of developing an implementation plan (the journey toward the goal) may have to be more flexible than establishing the goals (the destination):

- There are no established routes that will lead directly to the goal.

- There are many routes or methods that will enable us to reach the same destination.

- We may not have the knowledge to clearly identify all of the steps to achieve the goal.

- The steps to achieve the identified goal may have to evolve as the organization's climate changes.

In spite of this, utilize available information. At the same time, recognize that an implementation plan is a critical step in the goal-setting process.

In the implementation planning stage, there are other critical factors that we should also identify and include:

- The known or perceived hurdles that we must overcome. If there are impediments, they should be clearly identified, and a plan of action should be developed to overcome the challenges.

- The preparation necessary to accomplish the goals. The goals and the preparation needed for achievement must be in harmony. (**Preparation is discussed in Chapter 5.**)

- The people that are enablers and can assist us in accomplishing our goals. A critical step is to then begin developing relationships with these individuals. (**Relationships are discussed in Chapter 7.**)

- The major points along the way that can be measured and the time expected to be spent at each point.

If we fail to address any one of these factors, it can result in failure or, at the very minimum, delay the process.

I am often asked if there is a specific format that the implementation plan should follow. Since this plan is a personal document and seldom shared with others, the format can be very formal or just as informal as that developed when planning a vacation. Although my response may appear somewhat cavalier, I am more concerned with the content of the plan than the format.

Since maintaining an implementation plan is not a static process, we must continuously evaluate, reassess, and alter it as the environment changes. The plan must be both flexible and adjustable. Regardless of the amount of information readily available, we must continuously evaluate it for relevance. Likewise, we must continuously incorporate or clarify the steps as circumstances or environments change, time passes, the goal becomes more in focus, or more information becomes available. Just as ants make adjustments to meet specific environmental conditions, we must be just as diligent in making adjustments to our implementation plan.

> **The astronauts going to the moon were off course 90% of the time. They constantly had to adjust their course to reach their goal.**
>
> —Dorothy Wagner, PhD, US psychotherapist

My Struggle to Establish Realistic Goals

My initial attempt at developing goals along with an implementation plan was not as easy or complete as outlined above. After I completed my undergraduate degree, I established a personal goal for a career in a corporation. Although my goal was very simplistic, it was based on the valid information available to me at that time. The goal was "To Become a Success in Corporate America." Looking back, my goal was not very specific since I did not define success. I had no experience or personal knowledge of corporations except as defined in a theoretical textbook. In addition, there were few African Americans as role models. The steps and implementation plan were almost nonexistent since my goal was established during a time when African Americans were just beginning to enter the professional ranks of corporations in large numbers. Once I gathered more personal information, my goals, steps, and implementation plan were all revised and became much more specific. The revised goal was

"To Become a Senior Executive in a Fortune 50 Corporation." Although this goal was perceived to be a stretch, and some counseled me that it was unrealistic, I refused to change my goal. Rather than becoming disenchanted by the naysayers or being deterred by the negativism, I began preparation for my journey. It was obvious to me that I needed additional grooming, training, broadening experiences, and external support. All of these items were included in my Steps or implementation plan.

After receiving my Certified Public Accountant (CPA) certification, I had several lucrative opportunities, but they were not in corporations and ran counter to my personal goal. My major decision at the time was whether I should abandon my long-term goal for some early rewards or continue the pursuit. In spite of what appeared to be significant short-term opportunities, they were not part of the plan, and I was unwilling to change direction. My guiding principles were to remain focused, maintain singleness of purpose, and remain committed to my long-term goal.

Yes, I achieved my goal of becoming a senior executive in corporate America at a relatively young age. Some may ask, "Was the goal I established too low?" Although it is a logical question, I will never be able to honestly answer since it was clearly a huge stretch goal when I established it. However, with that goal accomplished, I have subsequently established additional goals outside of corporations and continue to work toward their achievement.

Lesson on Stretch Goals

Always establish stretch goals. Do not be deterred by naysayers, do not allow short-term success to derail you, and stay focused on your long-term goals as long as the passion remains. However, once the long-term goals are attained, celebrate the success, and remember there are always many other goals to accomplish.

Developing goals and outlining an implementation plan provide the destination and the roadmap for the journey. The success or failure in attaining these goals will then be determined by the level of commitment we make. There will be hurdles, obstacles, and detours along the way. Remember the hurdles of the desert ants? When these hurdles are encountered, we must maintain a singleness of purpose. We can and should be willing to adjust our direction while maintaining focus on the destination.

Although goals are important, maintaining a positive attitude is required, and ensuring commitment is essential to achieve success. There are many factors that can impede progress in goal attainment:

- **Lack of Focus**—We must consistently keep our effort focused on the goal or the destination we established. Maintain focus to avoid drifting, losing direction, and failing in our effort.

- **Incomplete Implementation Plan**—If we fail to develop an implementation plan, we increase the likelihood of meandering and not directing our efforts toward our goal. Even if we are working diligently but the energy is misdirected, the effort is futile. We must always make sure that the implementation plan is complete, updated timely, and that progress toward accomplishment is continuously measured.

- **Allowing Others to Change the Direction**—Recognize that others may attempt to change our direction. They may attempt to redirect our efforts to further their personal goals, to point us in the direction they believe important, or just to derail success. Accept input, advice, and counsel, but keep the goal in focus. Change direction only after careful consideration of all factors.

- **Lack of Commitment**—Even though the goals may be laser clear and the implementation plan thorough, we can be easily derailed unless we have total commitment. Accomplishing goals requires commitment as well as an unyielding quest for success.

- **Unrealistic Goals**—If we have unrealistic goals, we dramatically increase our potential for failure. Let's give ourselves at least a fair chance and be realistic in the expectations. Establish goals that are realistic but attainable with considerable effort and appropriate preparation.

Planning or establishing goals is something that we do regularly for our personal lives. However, we do not always equate this planning to goal setting. How many times have we gotten on a bus and said we are going wherever the bus takes us? How many times have we started on an extended vacation without a plan? Instead, we identify our destination and plan the route that will get us to the destination easily. That is the essence of establishing goals and developing an implementation plan.

Much has been written about the necessity of establishing goals and focusing effort on accomplishing those goals. The reason for the volumes of information on the subject is that it is one of the most critical determinants of success. Just as we would not go on vacation without a plan, we should not begin our career without a plan.

> Give me a stock clerk with a goal, and I will give you a man who will make history. Give me a man without a goal, and I will give you a stock clerk.

—James Cash Penney (1875–1971), founder, J. C. Penney Company

Establishing goals and ensuring their accomplishment are essential for success, but this process is not limited to humans. Insects and other animals are just as focused in their commitment to accomplishing goals. The tenacity with which ants seek and accomplish their goals is nothing short of remarkable. Our quest in seeking and accomplishing our personal goals should be just as focused as, and should match or exceed, that of these insects.

My interest is in the future ... because I am going
to spend the rest of my life there. That is my reason
for planning.

—Charles F. Kettering (1876–1958),
US engineer and cofounder of Sloan-Kettering Institute for Cancer Research

Chapter Four

Self-Development and Peregrine Falcons

The secret of success in life is for a man to be
ready for his opportunity when it comes.

—Benjamin Disraeli (1804–1881), British prime minister and statesman

PRINCIPLE FOUR

Pursue Competence, Develop Marketable Skills,
Polish Image, and Practice Professionalism.

The Peregrine Falcon's Development

Peregrine falcons are well known for their tremendous speed, spectacular dives, and extraordinary success in hunting. However, less is known about the huge preparation required to develop their skills. Since they rely solely on individual performance for food to sustain life, they are taught before they leave their parents' side the art of hunting. They spend up to two months (a significant amount of time in a falcon's life) practicing, learning the nuances of judgment, observing mock chases, and receiving coaching from their parents. They develop these hunting skills to survive and flourish. The tutelage, imitations, observations, and practice prepare peregrine falcons for the success that they achieve later in life.

Lesson Inspired by Nature

You must demonstrate the same level of dedication and commitment to self-development as that exhibited by peregrine falcons. Invest the necessary time, effort, and commitment since personal self-development is the key to your success.

There are no secrets to success. It is the result of preparation, hard work, and learning from failures.

—Colin L. Powell, secretary of state and US Army general

Managing Development

It would be remarkable if we could perform extraordinary feats with no preparation. Unfortunately, we were not placed on this earth with all of the skills necessary to always perform effectively. Because of this lack of skills, we must pursue the personal development that is necessary to efficiently perform our daily tasks. We develop some skills naturally as we progress from childhood to adulthood. Just as peregrine falcons do, we learn other skills based on environmental factors and other extensive preparation. Development is a continuous process that we must pursue throughout a lifetime if we are to adapt to the ever-changing environment.

Career self-development consists of acquiring skills, competencies, and related experiences necessary to perform effectively in our chosen organizations. We must not limit ourselves to merely the development of technical skills. Instead, we should strive for growth and excellence of the total person. We must pursue the tasks of growing, preparing to accept, and effectively performing more challenging assignments. Self-development must be a high personal priority, managed effectively, and never left to chance. Since we are the CEOs of our careers, we must manage these careers as our personal companies.

> To develop ourselves is life's greatest
> and noblest project.
>
> —Alfred A. Montapert, US motivational author

With the proliferation of outsourcing, right-sourcing, downsizing, and other challenges, it is highly unlikely that most individuals will remain with a single professional organization for a lifetime. While this may still occasionally occur, the frequency has decreased significantly. We should never plan our development expecting to remain in one organization for our entire career. Prepare for the eventuality that tomorrow we may be in an organization experiencing turmoil and be forced to market our skills to another professional organization. Our objective should be to always stay prepared for that eventuality but not be paranoid about the possibility. If we direct time and effort toward ensuring complete self-development, we will be prepared for any possibility.

Promotion Denied

Larry, a personal friend, told the story of what gave him the motivation for self-development. During his undergraduate years, he was a star athlete, fraternity member, and honor student in a large university. After graduating and spending a number of years in his chosen organization, Larry was denied a much sought-after promotion. He was told that he was not selected because he was not adequately prepared to take on the responsibility of the position. Although the oversight was a disappointment, the rationale for the decision deflated his ego. Even though accepting the rejection was difficult and could have been defeating, Larry viewed it as a challenge and vowed that never again would anyone ever be able to use preparation as a reason to deny him a promotion. He subsequently sought and received his Certified Public Accountant (CPA) certification, Master's in Business Administration (MBA), and a law degree while working full time and raising a family. Needless to say, preparation was never again an issue, and Larry subsequently became a senior executive in a major organization.

Lesson on Preparation

Always survey your organization's environment, identify the requirements, and make sure you are prepared for opportunities as they become available. Never allow lack of preparation to be the factor that hinders your career progress.

Self-development has both performance and physical dimensions. The performance dimensions relate primarily to career preparation while the physical dimensions relate to personal development.

Performance Dimensions—We must remain diligent, seek to excel, and always be prepared to accept more complex assignments or projects as they become available. To accomplish this, we must continuously (1) develop transferable skills, (2) receive appropriate training, (3) accept developmental assignments, (4) consider promotional opportunities, (5) avoid misguided promotions, (6) accept lateral assignments, and (7) consider organizational change.

> **Nothing ever comes to one, that is worth having, except as a result of hard work.**
>
> —Booker T. Washington (1856–1915),
> inventor, political activist, and educator

❖ **Transferable Skills**—Job security and even organizational structures are uniquely different from those seen years ago. There is much more uncertainty as to when an organization will be required to adjust its employee level just to remain competitive. Because of the uncertainty, it is essential that skills developed are broad based and transferable to other organizations. Yes, many organizations have a number of one-of-a-kind positions that are unique to that organization. However, in these unique positions, the skills gained are not transferable and can only be utilized in that organization. We must never allow ourselves to be shuttled off permanently into a one-of-a-kind position unless it is to gain essential knowledge. Even then, there should be an agreed exit strategy. Although the one-of-a-kind position could allow for the development of unique expertise and could potentially provide organizational longevity, there is no certainty. It substantially reduces our marketability and leaves us extremely vulnerable to the organization. The skills we develop must be applicable and useful to many organizations, and the one-of-a-kind position does not pass the transferable-skills test. It is our responsibility to stay in the mainstream and develop transferable skills. It allows us to continue progressing in our current organization or to move easily into another organization if an unexpected change is required or if we choose to seek opportunities elsewhere.

> ## Luck is what happens when preparation meets opportunity.
>
> —Elmer G. Letterman

❖ **Training**—Regardless of the talent or the skills we bring into an organization, both continuous growth and development are essential for advancement. Remember peregrine falcons? They rely on their internal training for survival. Since most organizations are genuinely interested in the development of their employees, they sometimes offer internal training opportunities. Always be an advocate for the training and additional exposure available through internal programs. This is not to imply that internal training will never be provided unless we advocate, but it is our responsibility to determine our development needs and ensure that we are given fair consideration. It should never be left to chance. Based on our personal assessment of weaknesses and developmental needs, we may also require other external training and development to enhance skills or complement the internal training base. Never hesitate to be an advocate for this training. If the external training is considered essential and we cannot get organizational support, we must pursue self-development regardless of how it is achieved.

❖ **Developmental Assignments**—Many organizations provide developmental assignments, which are opportunities designed for the sole purpose of preparing the individual for broader responsibilities. These opportunities are designed to provide additional work-related, contact-related, or skills-related exposure to enhance preparation for more challenging opportunities. Some of these assignments may even be created to address a specific need. However, they may not necessarily be labeled as developmental. Be aware that all of our needs are not always apparent to us, and every reference to a developmental assignment is not a criticism of our performance. These positions are often necessary for continuous growth and should be viewed positively. Additionally, since we are aware of our long-term goals and know our current preparation, we must be advocates for the development we believe necessary. When presented with such an opportunity, we should seek appropriate counsel, discuss the rationale or expected personal benefit, and recognize that developmental assignments or broadening experiences can pay huge dividends.

❖ **Promotional Opportunities**—In most cases, our promotional opportunities will result from organizational growth, retirements, or other personnel changes. Our objectives should be to ensure that we are considered for promotional opportunities on par with or above that of our contemporaries. If we are not considered, we must understand why and determine if we must seek additional preparation or personal development. We must always indicate our willingness to accept additional challenges. It is a passive approach to patiently sit and quietly wait for promotions to just happen since, as we know, few positive things happen in life without intervention. Instead, we must be advocates, be prepared, and make sure that the decision makers are aware of our interests in being considered for advancement opportunities.

❖ **Misguided Promotions**—Unless we are willing to change our goals, we must be prepared to reject promotions if they are completely at odds with our established goals or implementation plans. Often, the promotions that appear to be opportunities for advancement can provide short-term gains but will not move us toward our long-term goals. We must always keep focused on our goals, avoid being sidetracked, and maintain our direction.

A Rejected Promotion

I was once offered a promotion that caused me considerable concern. The position included a significant reward financially, but the location was in a remote area of Alaska. Because there was insufficient infrastructure, my family would not have been located near the job location. Additionally, the work schedule required two weeks of continuous work followed by two weeks off to spend with family. Although some advised me that the financial rewards were too good to reject and I was unwise to reject such a lucrative offer, I decided not to accept the promotion. My reasons were as follows:

- A desire to maintain a close-knit family structure

- A desire to maintain a balanced life

- A fear of being organizationally isolated

- A concern that the position was not consistent with my long-term goals

Since I viewed this position as inconsistent with family life and professional goals, I was willing to reject it and live with the consequences.

Lesson on Promotional Advancement

Always balance the short-term benefits of a potential promotion with your long-term goals. What initially may be viewed as progress could be, in reality, a monumental step in the wrong direction.

❖ **Lateral Assignments**—Often, a change in position, location, or organization may be necessary to reach the identified goal. A lateral move is an assignment to a similar position, a position with a similar scope, or a position with comparable responsibilities in the same organization. In today's environment, the labor market is shrinking, there are fewer management positions available, and there are fewer layers in most organizations. Because of this, it may be necessary to accept a lateral move if our goals require a broad range of skills that can be best obtained by exposure in different positions. However, it is always important to maintain focus on the long-term goal rather than having angst about the short-term position.

My Foreign Assignment

I was confronted with a difficult decision that involved a developmental assignment, a lateral move, and a significant relocation. The decision was made more difficult because the opportunity came at a time when our children were in the preteen and teen years. After progressing steadily through the organization, I was offered a position in a foreign country. Although not specifically identified as such, the assignment was clearly a lateral move for developmental purposes, and it also required the relocation of my entire family to an unknown land. In addition to the family considerations, I had questions:

- Would this assignment aid in helping me reach my long-term goal?

- Was it an experience that I needed to continue my advancement and to eventually break through the glass ceiling?

Major issues were that the parent company was foreign, the opportunity was in the headquarter's office, and the potential exposure was excellent. After careful consideration and thorough discussion with my family and certain members of my network, I accepted the assignment. I accepted the assignment for four basic reasons:

- It was an opportunity to showcase my skills and readiness for increased responsibility.

- The skills I would learn during an international experience would improve my internal opportunities and definitely be transferable to other organizations.

- Similar opportunities had been offered to others within the organization for the purpose of assessing their readiness for more advanced opportunities.

- Broad-based experience was clearly critical for me to reach my long-term goal.

Because of these factors, I disrupted family routines, and we relocated for a two-and-one-half year period. In retrospect, this was probably one of my most important career decisions. Even though the position was at best a lateral, it provided me with the opportunity to develop relationships with additional key decision makers in the organization. Just as the tutelage, observations, and practice prepare peregrine falcons for their success, this assignment was instrumental in preparing me for future assignments. It was a period of tremendous personal growth since the position provided the opportunity to work on projects with people from around the world. However, the telltale sign that the decision had been pivotal became apparent when subsequent opportunities became available upon my return to the United States.

Lesson: Lateral Assignments

Sometimes lateral assignments are for developmental purposes. Often, they provide the skills, exposure, or training necessary for advancement. However, we should examine each opportunity carefully, understand the benefits, and recognize the potential risks before beginning the journey.

❖ **Organizational Change**—Sometimes, we may find it extremely difficult or even impossible to achieve our identified goals in our current organization. Often, our goals may be counter-culture to the organization, or the decision makers may fail to recognize our talents, skills, or ambitions. For example, the goal could be to become an effective career manager in a legal or accounting partnership. However, these organizations may not have positions for career managers. If we encounter such a situation, the decision then becomes whether we should change goals or change organizations. A change in organizations is often the more realistic solution, even though circumstances may dictate status quo. Regardless of the final decision, we should weigh the advantages and disadvantages. We can then make an informed decision if we know the organization's limitations and the requirements to accomplish our goals.

Making Another Choice

My first professional opportunity after undergraduate school was in a sales environment. After progressing through all of the phases of the training program, I was identified as a candidate for the next available store manager opening. Although I had worked hard, received several awards, and progressed rapidly, I was not enjoying my career and was just not having fun. For an extended period, I expressed an interest in changing direction in the organization, but management would not consider that alternative.

After I submitted a letter of resignation, local, regional, and national management suddenly began considering me for other positions. At that time, I was offered a choice of several positions to encourage me to stay with the organization. However, I had made my decision and rejected all considerations. My major issue was the organization's lack of concern for me and my interests. I also wondered why a letter of resignation was the only way to be heard by the decision makers. Needless to say, I left that organization, joined another, and never second-guessed my decision.

Lesson: Organizational Change

Do not be disenchanted if an organization fails to recognize your talents or skills. Stay focused on your goals, keep performing, and seek another organization that will value you and your contributions.

Developing professionally is our individual responsibility. Yes, we may get support, just as the peregrine falcon is given support, but we must devote the time and effort to ensuring our development. We will be provided with opportunities for growth and challenge when we develop transferable skills, obtain appropriate training, pursue developmental assignments, and accept promotional opportunities. This will not only prepare us to meet our long-term goals, it will also provide us with continued challenges, which makes for a more fulfilling career.

Physical Dimensions—Even though there are just as many physical aspects to self-development as there are performance aspects, in this context, I will focus on (1) physical attire, (2) physical appearance, and (3) office conduct.

> ## Learn the art of dressing well, otherwise you will not sell for what you are worth.
>
> —Dorothy Wagner, PhD, US psychotherapist

❖ **Physical Attire**—Maintaining appropriate physical attire at all times is a critical part of self-development. The organization's culture often dictates whether the appropriate attire is casual or more traditional. Regardless of the expectations, smart, conservative attire is never wrong. Yes, I have heard the argument that performance assessments should not be based on the clothes we wear. I have also heard the argument that attire does not affect job performance. While these arguments have merit and are theoretically sound, in reality, physical attire does matter, and it does enter into the decision-making process. In spite of the ever-changing organizational landscape, it is still impossible to eliminate physical attire from consideration when comparing individuals for advancement. We may never hear a word spoken about what is appropriate or inappropriate or even how others perceive our physical attire. However, be aware that observations are always being made, stored for future reference, and used in the assessment process. The reason physical attire is important is that an employee represents the organization to the community, customers, and other internal and external contacts. That representation is vital to the organization's image. Additionally, we are marketing ourselves at all times, and how we package the product (ourselves) is critical for long-term success. Maintaining the appropriate dress code or physical attire at all times is essential.

> **Poise is a big factor in a man's success. If I were a young man just starting out I would talk things over with myself as a friend. I would set out to develop poise—for it can be developed. A man should learn to stand, what to do with his hands, what to do with his feet, look another straight in the eye, dress well and look well and know he looks well. By dressing well, I don't mean expensively, but neatly and in good taste.**
>
> —F. Edson White, president, Armour and Company Merchants

❖ **Physical Appearance**—The term physical appearance refers primarily to our external deportment, the way we carry ourselves, and our demeanor. Not only is our verbal communication important, but the information we communicate about ourselves nonverbally also leaves a lasting impression. Physical appearance as discussed here includes attitude, hygiene, our walk, our expressions, and everything else about us. It relates to the external perceptions, either positive or negative, we leave with others we meet. Maintaining the appropriate physical appearance is a major aspect of self-development that will not be openly discussed, yet the expectation is that we will maintain excellent physical appearance at all times. We must continuously focus on our physical attributes to ensure that our external facade does not conflict with the organization's culture. This is not implying or suggesting, in any manner, that we deny ethnic heritage or change our personality. However, it is implying that, as we celebrate our heritage, we celebrate it in a professional manner.

❖ **Office Conduct**—The manner in which we conduct ourselves in a work environment will have a significant impact on the ability to reach our long-term goals. Conduct is important for many reasons; most importantly it

- Telegraphs to others how we want to be treated in the work environment;

- Demonstrates to others the level of our trustworthiness;

- Identifies the level of our professionalism;

- Indicates the level of commitment we are making to the organization;

- Indicates our ability to manage ourselves.

We must make a clear distinction between the work environment and our social environment. I am not suggesting that we should not socialize in the work environment, but recognize that certain forms of conduct that are acceptable in a social environment may not be appropriate in a professional or work environment.

In many organizations, there is a written code of conduct. However, in all organizations, there is an unwritten code that all employees are expected to observe. Accepting and adhering to the written code is relatively straightforward. The expectations are clearly identified, they can be understood, and a pattern can be developed to ensure compliance. Although customs are not as straightforward, they are just as significant because they also define expectations. Even though customs are unwritten, their significance is not diminished. Unfortunately, these customs can only be learned through observation or by communication with other employees. Regardless of whether written or unwritten, it is important that we maintain a professional attitude or approach in the work environment. We must learn self-management techniques, practice self-control, and manage our behavior at all times.

Much is written about human needs for personal development to accomplish goals or objectives. However, little is written about a similar necessity for development in birds, insects, and animals. The developmental needs and preparation are just as valuable for the survival of many of these creatures as it is for our success. Our dedication to self-development should be just as persistent as that of the peregrine falcon so that we can enjoy the same level of success they achieve.

Whether or not you reach your goals in life depends entirely on how well you prepare for them and how badly you want them.

—Ronald McNair, PhD (1950–1986), US astronaut

Chapter Five

Work Ethic
and Beavers

Nothing in the world can take the place of persistence. Talent will not; nothing is more common than unsuccessful men with talent. Genius will not; unrewarded genius is almost a proverb. Education will not; the world is full of educated derelicts. Persistence and determination alone are omnipotent.

—Calvin Coolidge (1872–1933), US president and politician

PRINCIPLE FIVE
Recognize That Motivated, Disciplined, Committed, and Persistent Performance Is Essential.

The Work Ethic of Beavers

We have all heard the saying, "Busy as a beaver," but we may not appreciate the significance of the comment. The unyielding determination and persistent performance distinguish beavers' work ethic from other animals. For all of their precision in constructing dams and building lodges, beavers use unusual features of their anatomy for these roles. They use their teeth to cut trees, have a unique ability to walk on their back legs, carry material between the surfaces of their front legs and chin, and use their powerful tails to pack material in place. Their work ethic is unmatched, especially when we consider their physical characteristics or limitations. Their work ethic and unique style distinguish them from all other rodents.

Lesson Inspired by Nature

Just as beavers have developed a dedicated and disciplined work ethic that distinguishes them from other rodents, you must develop a dedicated, disciplined, and persistent work ethic that distinguishes you from your peers.

> Genius is one percent inspiration and ninety-nine percent perspiration.
>
> —Thomas Alva Edison (1847–1931), US inventor

Dedication to Work Ethic

Developing and maintaining a strong, disciplined, and dedicated work ethic is one of the single most important factors in determining success. Work ethic is the philosophy, the principles, or the approach we take toward our individual performance. We have all seen individuals with what appeared to be similar educations, talents, and other skills. Often, one advances in the organization at a much faster pace than the other. We sometimes attribute the success to working hard. However, the employee's level of energy invested, the maximization of skills, and a strong work ethic are the major factors. Never perform an assignment with a carefree approach. Every task must be approached with dedication, discipline, and energy as if it is the only opportunity that will determine our success or failure. In Caroline V. Clark's *Take a Lesson: Today's Black Achievers on How They Made It and What They Learned along the Way*, Kenneth Chenault, CEO of American Express, told the following story. "Every morning in Africa, a gazelle wakes up. It knows it must run faster than the fastest cheetah, or it will be killed. Every morning in Africa, a cheetah wakes up. It knows it must outrun the slowest gazelle, or it will starve to death. It does not matter whether you are a cheetah, or a gazelle. When the sun comes up, you'd better be running." Many of our peers have the same mental attitude as the gazelle and the cheetah, If we are to be competitive and successful, we must be just as committed and willing to make the same type of investment for our careers.

Disciplined Work Ethic

Not surprisingly, a number of professionals I know enjoyed successful careers due to their unyielding determination and disciplined work ethic. When asked, they indicated that their strong work ethic was a product of their home, instilled by parents, or resulted from their close-knit environment. These were the most significant and most frequently stated factors motivating them to excel in their performance. Other professionals found it more difficult to identify the specific source but pointed to icons, stars, the desire for change, and other factors as providing their motivation. Regardless of the source or whether it was instilled, learned, developed, or self-generated, a strong, determined work ethic was evident and identified by these professionals as the reason for their success.

Lesson: Work Ethic

The work environment today is very competitive, especially with the globalization of professional organizations. Therefore, a strong and determined work ethic, directed toward excellent performance, is a prerequisite for your success.

For every one of us that succeeds, it's because there's somebody there to show you the way out. The light doesn't necessarily have to be in your family; for me it was teachers and school.

—Oprah Winfrey, US philanthropist, actress, and television producer.

In general, people are motivated by many different external factors including need, recognition, ambition, praise, anger, and hope. Similarly, people are de-motivated by many external factors including fear, anger, mistakes, mistreatment, lack of recognition, and discontentment. During our careers, we will likely experience some or all of these motivating and de-motivating factors. It is not difficult to focus on goals and minimize external distractions when experiencing motivating factors. However, because the environment is ever-changing, not all of our encounters will be positive. We must develop a self-generated, dedicated work ethic that is strong enough to withstand the de-motivating factors. We must have a strong internal desire to succeed. Avoid searching for external sources to buoy our confidence and provide the motivation to keep us focused. Recognize that life is really not as good as it seems on the best day, and it is clearly not as bad as it appears on the worst day.

Without a strong and disciplined work ethic, we remove the opportunity to even be considered for additional responsibility or promotional opportunities. Summarized below are some additional fundamental qualities to include in this disciplined work ethic, which are (1) self-motivation, (2) preparation, (3) performance, (4) commitment, (5) perseverance, (6) resilience, (7) thoroughness, (8) accountability, (9) professionalism, and (10) involvement.

Before everything else, getting ready is the secret of success.

—Henry Ford (1863–1947), founder, Ford Motor Company

❖ **Self-Motivation**—Often, actions are taken, issues resolved, and tasks completed because of a specific request, a requirement, or, external pressure. However, self-motivated individuals will accomplish many of these same tasks without external influences. The major factors affecting self-motivation are personal desire, internal drive, and the willingness to ensure successful performance regardless of the circumstances. Self-motivated individuals are self-starters. In many organizations, much of what is necessary for continued operations is undefined and, therefore, not included in a traditional position description. Self-motivation is needed to identify the requirements, to be a self-starter, and to perform the task without being directed. Self-motivation is not only necessary, it a prerequisite for leadership opportunities.

It is better to be prepared for an opportunity and not have one than to have an opportunity and not be prepared.

—Whitney Young (1921–1971),
executive director, National Urban League, and political activist

❖ **Preparation**—The term preparation implies that there must be a commitment to being ready for opportunities that may become available. Being prepared does not imply waiting for someone else to act or identify the necessary requirements. Instead, it requires initiative to recognize the organizational needs and ensure we are ready when these opportunities become available. To become a surgeon, physicist, lawyer, or skilled tradesman requires significant preparation before practicing the profession. Additionally, it requires maintaining knowledge of current developments within the profession or trade. So it is with most professions and in most organizations. I once heard a saying that has remained with me over the years. The saying is to always remember the six "P's" of preparation and use them as a guide in your chosen career. They are: "Prior Planning Prevents Progressively Poor Performance." If we expect to have stellar performance, we must be constantly prepared. We should not expect significant opportunities for advancement unless we have invested time and effort preparing ourselves.

Commitment to Preparation

When I received my undergraduate degree, I thought I had all of the formal training or preparation necessary for success. While it is conceivable that the skills were sufficient, I had not considered that there would be thirty other individuals in the department with similar skills. The realization struck me that, just as the beaver distinguishes itself from other rodents, I needed to distinguish myself from my contemporaries. Since being like everyone else was just not sufficient, I began additional preparation as a way of distinguishing myself. My initial quest was the Certified Public Accountant (CPA) certification, which is the quintessential proof of expertise in the accounting profession. Although being a lifelong accountant was not my goal, I was seeking an objective means to indicate expertise in the profession. This certificate of expertise was a way to eliminate potential excuses for not being considered for advancement. After completing the CPA certification, it was important to demonstrate that my interest and expertise expanded outside of the technical accounting field. I then pursued and completed my Master of Business Administration (MBA) degree. The question can be asked, "Was all of this necessary, or should everyone be expected to follow a similar path?" Clearly, the answer is no. It is difficult to outline the definitive criteria or the preparation necessary for success in any profession or organization since they are all different. My preparation and commitment proved to be well timed and clearly a worthy investment since it significantly enhanced my career possibilities.

> ## Lesson on Commitment
> It is necessary to assess the needs of your profession and organization, determine the personal development required, prepare yourself, and commit to a strong work ethic. This preparation will enable you to seize the opportunity when it becomes available.

Plan purposefully, prepare prayerfully, proceed positively, and pursue persistently.

—William A. Ward (1921–1994),
US author, religious leader, educator, and teacher

❖ **Performance**—Any discussion of work ethic must include performance as one of the fundamental principles. Remember the work ethic of beavers? Their ongoing performance and commitment is unmatched. Performance commitment is the responsibility to do the very best job possible and give nothing short of 100% effort in every assignment. The underlying assumption is that performance will be consistent, stellar, and that there will be effective completion of every project assigned. Remove all thoughts of performing at the top level on only the perceived high-profile projects. The approach should always be that every task, regardless of how insignificant it may appear, is the most important task in the organization. Of course, we all know that every assignment will not be the most important, but our mindset should always be the same. Since there is no reduction in pay for the perceived less-important projects or increase in pay for the high-profile ones, there should be no difference in the commitment. My philosophy has always been very simple: "Work for every day paid, get paid for every day worked and, at the end, there are no IOUs on anyone's part." Always be able to look back and be comfortable with the effort on every task. Never be in a position where others question your commitment, dedication, or performance regardless of the visibility, the significance, or in spite of the adversity.

> **Don't bother just to be better than your contemporaries or predecessors. Try to be better than yourself.**
>
> —William Faulkner (1897–1962), Nobel Prize–winning fiction novelist

The performance of other employees should not be the barometer that determines our effort, nor should we allow others to impact the level of our effort. Note that beavers do not use other rodents as their benchmark. We are never sure how others' performance is regarded by decision makers. Additionally, we may be establishing low standards by using underachievers as our benchmark. Insisting on consistent stellar performance does not imply that we can never make mistakes. We are all human and capable of mistakes. However, we must always be diligent students, learn, and use our mistakes as instruments for growth rather than symbols of failure.

A dedication to superior performance is essential since there will often be adversity and even failure in spite of our best effort. It is during adverse conditions that our steadfastness of purpose must continue to guide us toward the completion of tasks. Our objective should be to maintain top level performance even during these difficult times.

If you don't make a total commitment to whatever you're doing, then you start looking to bail out the first time the boat starts leaking.

—Lou Holtz, professional football coach

❖ **Commitment**—Commitment is the determination or stick-to-itiveness we maintain in pursuing a task, an issue, an assignment, or a career. It is the investment of our time, our effort, our level of dedication, our persistence, and our enthusiasm to accomplish our goals. There is a significant amount of truth in the saying that we only get out of life what we are willing to put into it—no more or no less. The potential for achievement is relatively remote if we are not committed, if we are unwilling to make a significant investment to excel in our performance, or if we unenthusiastically pursue the accomplishment of our goals.

Commitment also requires both positive and negative risks. The positive risk is that others will recognize our commitment and be willing to reward us with additional responsibility or advancement. The additional opportunities may be earlier than expected or exceed our preparation, but they are opportunities for advancement. We also risk that decision makers may not recognize and reward our dedicated or committed effort. However, these positive and negative risks are no greater, nor any less, than those we face in our personal lives. We must overcome the lack of security or the uncertainty and demonstrate dedication and perseverance. However, if our commitment is not recognized, we must definitely consider whether our personal goals and the organization's plans for us are appropriately aligned.

On Commitment

I am reminded of a commitment my daughter made at a very young age. Since her school did not offer a soccer sports program, the parents of a classmate asked her to join a soccer travel team. Because she had not played competitively, her early excitement was quickly replaced with uncertainty. After a few days of hot summer practices, she approached me saying she wanted to quit the team. Her reason was, "Everybody is better than I am." We talked about her concern, the commitment she made to the team, and the importance of keeping her word. She agreed to complete the season and give 100% effort. We agreed that if she felt that same way at the end of the season, she could quit at that time. However, during the season, she developed a real love for the game, dedicated herself to improving performance, and became a solid, consistent player. Over the next few years, she continued to perform and showed the dedication, commitment, willingness, and energy toward continuously improving performance. The reward for her commitment was being competitively selected to the state Junior Olympic Team for the under-fourteen age group.

That same commitment was again demonstrated during her brief years in a professional organization. Although her undergraduate training was not business related, she progressed rapidly because of the commitment to a strong work ethic, willingness to invest time, and dedicated effort toward continuous improvement. She is now completing graduate work at the University of Chicago. Her commitment has been similar to that as a child in soccer and as an adult in a major corporate organization. Her accomplishments did not result from extraordinary skills or abilities, but from her strong commitment to performing well on the tasks she faced.

Lesson: Success Is Available

Success is not reserved for the most likely candidate, the person with the early preparation, or the person with the most experience. It is available if you prepare yourself and remain committed to excellent performance at all times.

❖ **Perseverance**—Perseverance is the ability or the drive to continue steadfastly with a task until its completion. Just as the beaver colony builds its dams, perseverance involves staying focused on the overall objective and overcoming any obstacles that may be encountered. It means refusing to accept defeat, maintaining stick-to-itiveness, and adopting a "don't-give-up" attitude. Perseverance is critical since competition is keen, there will be many challenges, and often progress may appear distant. The effort must be based on high moral standards, directed toward personal goals, and guided by organizational objectives. Perseverance is maintaining self-confidence, staying focused on the goal, and forging ahead without hesitation.

On Perseverance

Perhaps one of the more well-known examples of perseverance is that shown by Abraham Lincoln:

- Failed in business in 1831 and again in 1833.

- Defeated for the legislature in 1832.

- Suffered a nervous breakdown in 1836.

- Defeated for speaker in 1838 and for elector in 1840.

- Defeated for congressional nomination in 1843.

- Defeated for Congress in 1848 and for the Senate in 1855.

- Defeated for vice president in 1858.

- Elected president of the United States in 1860.

Although it took thirty years, his perseverance enabled him to reach the highest elected office in the United States.

Lesson on Perseverance

Never give up on your dreams. If you maintain the same level of perseverance as Abraham Lincoln and continuously stay focused on your goals, there is no question that success will be yours.

❖ **Resilience**—We will encounter many challenges and some setbacks regardless of the organization, the level of preparation, or the circumstances in life. It does not matter how much planning, preparation, or care we take, not every opportunity will be successful. It does not matter our position, our status, or our career, impediments are inevitable. The measure of success is not the number of setbacks but the consistency with which we rebound. We must maintain the strength to continue progressing toward our goals in spite of the difficulties.

Fall seven times; stand up eight.

—Ancient Chinese Proverb

❖ **Thoroughness**—Thoroughness is the patience to review all aspects of an issue or project prior to making a final decision. It is avoiding shortcuts just to complete a task. It is the investment we make to ensure the accuracy, precision, and completeness of a task. It is the ambition, the determination, the energy, and the drive to exceed performance expectations. Being thorough does not imply that we should be excessive in our effort and find ourselves in "analysis-paralysis." This can be just as detrimental since it is often viewed as overanalyzing, being anal retentive, detail oriented, or reluctant to make a decision. Being excessive has tremendous downsides. Thoroughness suggests that we carefully review all pertinent issues, understand the implications, and avoid shortcuts. A lack of thoroughness adversely affects the level of our performance and negatively impacts the achievement of our goals.

> **I do the very best I know how—the very best I can; and I mean to keep on doing so until the end.**
>
> —Abraham Lincoln (1809–1865), US president and politician

❖ **Accountability**—Accountability is the willingness to accept personal responsibility for the performance and decisions made in executing our duties. It is the capacity to be forthright, even when circumstances, if left unexplained, could implicate others. It is the forthrightness to take personal responsibility regardless of the success or failure of the project. Often, we see individuals who quickly seek recognition for the successful projects but distance themselves from those less successful, even though they are directly responsible. It is inevitable that we will all have some successes and some failures throughout our careers. Because of this inevitability, we gain stature with decision makers, gain respect from peers, and show our integrity to all when we are accountable for our actions.

> **No matter how small and unimportant what we are doing may seem, if we do it well, it may soon become the step that will lead us to better things.**
>
> —Channing Pollock (1880–1946),
> US writer and playwright

❖ **Professionalism**—Professionalism is the care we take in completing a project and the manner in which we conduct ourselves during the process. Regardless of our personal belief of a project's significance, professionalism must be shown at all times. We also demonstrate our ability by the professionalism of the output. Since output is often the only means of demonstrating our performance, we must take extreme care with the final presentation. Even if we do stellar work in developing the project, if the final presentation is unprofessional or substandard, the perception will be that the overall performance is substandard. The final presentation will be viewed as an indication of how thorough the work on the project was performed. The extra time we take to make sure the final output is complete and professionally presented will play a major role in determining our success.

> **Remember, every time you open your mouth to talk, your mind walks out and parades up and down the words.**
>
> —Eric H. Stuart

❖ **Involvement**—Involvement means that we must stay connected with the activities and debates within the organization. The involvement indicates our personal interest, allows for positive contributions, and demonstrates our commitment to the overall team performance. It is particularly important to be actively involved on topics in which we have significant expertise. We must let our voices be heard. If we remain uninvolved, it not only robs the organization of valuable input but represents a lost opportunity to market our personal skills. A significant distinction is being made here between value-added and non-value-added involvement. Involvement where we add value is critical for success. However, active participation without adding value can be more damaging to our careers than a lack of involvement. When used wisely, active involvement is important to continued advancement.

Work ethic is one of the most fundamental and essential traits required for success in every endeavor or organization. It is important that we build and maintain a work ethic based on committed stellar performance, unyielding perseverance, determined thoroughness, dedicated accountability, and unrelenting professionalism. Avoiding or minimizing any of these qualities will likely jeopardize the accomplishment of goals.

We are sometimes faced with circumstances where our preparation, talents, or physical skills are not ideal for the task. However, note how beavers adapt to their environment and how their work ethic is more critical than their apparent anatomic features. Similarly, if we adopt the fundamental qualities discussed in this chapter, maintain commitment, and develop a strong, disciplined work ethic, we will be just as effective as beavers. These qualities will distinguish us from our contemporaries and assist in the accomplishment of our goals.

Success is dependent on effort.

—Sophocles (496–406 BC), Greek writer, philosopher, and playwright

Chapter Six

Attitude and Dolphins

Nothing can stop the man with the right mental
attitude from achieving his goals; nothing on earth
can help the man with the wrong attitude.

—W. E. Ziege

PRINCIPLE SIX
Understand That Success or Failure Is an Attitudinal Issue.

The Positive Attitude of Dolphins

We are all familiar with dolphins' sociability, affection, charm, intelligence, showmanship, and their tremendous tolerance and trust of humans. However, in the wild, these mammals are also noted for their adaptability and their ability to fend off predators while living in a hostile environment. Regardless of environmental factors, it is difficult to quell their resourcefulness since their gregariousness is the method often utilized for protection. In a captive environment or when they are not performing for an audience, dolphins maintain a positive attitude. They entertain themselves with formation swimming, synchronized leaping, acrobatic flips, and other playful acts. The continuous positive attitude, regardless of the environmental concerns, is always present in dolphins.

Lesson Inspired by Nature

To ensure success in your organization, you must maintain the same positive attitude as that exhibited by dolphins. Never allow the environment, critics, or other factors to negatively affect your attitude or the pursuit of your goals.

Think you can, think you can't; either way you will be right.

—Henry Ford (1863–1947), founder, Ford Motor Company

80

A Positive Attitude

We should never underestimate the importance or the impact that attitude has on success or failure. Attitude is the way we think or believe about life or even particular circumstances in life. It is instrumental in determining how we project ourselves and the approach we take in our decision making and daily activities. The quality of our decision making is affected by a positive or negative personal attitude. It is important that we focus our effort on maintaining a mental attitude that will positively affect performance and improve the quality of our lives.

The Power of a Positive Attitude

I was asked to create an organizational structure to provide critical administrative services to over 100,000 employees in over 800 locations throughout the United States. This daunting responsibility was made more difficult by the fact that these services had historically been provided by employees under the direct supervision of localized management. For local management, this change resulted in the loss of responsibility, a reduction in the size of the workforce, a reduced span of control, and a loss of perceived power. Obviously, this left many senior-level personnel in the organization with a negative feeling that manifested itself in many subliminal ways. Even though some initially raised legitimate concerns about the quality of services provided by my new organization, many made frivolous complaints.

There were some very difficult days for me personally. I found it imperative to search internally for strength to maintain a positive attitude and prevent the negativism from affecting my performance. Many executives within the organization privately told me, "You have the worst job in the organization. You been set up for failure." Sometimes it did seem that way. It would have been extremely easy for me to accept the comments, buy into the negativism, believe the undertones, and allow the environment to affect my performance. However, it was during this assignment that my belief in the significance of maintaining a positive attitude was reconfirmed. I was relatively new to the organization, unaware of the internal politics, and had not developed internal networks or other support systems. Although there were few external positive reinforcements, my firm belief was that continued performance and time were the only factors that would change these perceptions. Fortunately, after several years of struggle, we were able to manage the negativism, gain the respect of the organization members, and achieve success. However, without my internally generated positive attitude and confidence, the success that my group attained on this assignment would not have been possible. As a fitting conclusion, we received one of the highest awards offered by the organization for the achievement and for the tremendous impact this project had on the organization.

Lesson: Avoid Negative Influences

You cannot always depend on external factors or reinforcement to develop, promote, or maintain a positive attitude. Your positive attitude must be internally built, centrally fed, and personally guarded against external negative forces.

Men can alter their lives by altering their attitude.

—William James (1843–1916), US psychologist and philosopher

Success is dependent upon the attitude we maintain on a daily basis. This attitude is a determinant of how we carry ourselves, react to others, and project ourselves. If we maintain a positive attitude, we project that image and others observe, react, and respond in accordance with our actions. Remember how dolphins project an image that is positive? Since others perceive us in the manner we project and treat us the way we show them we want to be treated, we should project a positive image at all times. A positive attitude determines the level and quality of our interaction with others. The quality of our interaction with others is essential for our success.

> **Our attitudes control our lives. Attitudes are a secret power working twenty-four hours a day for good or bad. It is of paramount importance that we know how to harness and control this great force.**
>
> —Tom Blandi

A Smile in Your Voice

To provide high-quality support to employees, we needed a centralized employee service center. We designed the center to receive calls from around the country to resolve employee issues. When determining the project scope, it was clear that there were three critical factors necessary for success:

- **Technology**—This could be acquired or developed to suit the needs of the center.

- **Information**—This could be gathered and made available in an easily accessible manner with considerable effort.

- **People**—The most critical element of the project. Selection and training thus became a major focus.

The selection criteria I established was that only people with a smile in their voices should be considered for employment. The rationale was that, although technology and information were important, the personal contact was the critical success factor. Since there was no face contact and we were asking our customers to change their habits, it was essential that our call center personnel project a favorable image. The inside joke often heard on calls into the center was, "Let me hear that smile in your voice." The call center became a huge success, and the chief executive officer complimented the employees for their professionalism, attitude, and support. The success can be attributed to the caring attitude of the call center employees and the manner in which their positive attitude was projected to others.

Lesson: Keep a Smile in Your Voice

It is important to always maintain a positive attitude. The smile in your voice may be that extra quality needed to ensure success in your career.

Our attitudes are extremely important; we become what we dwell upon. If we dwell on adverse conditions, we intensify the bad. A man will remain a rag-picker as long as he has only that vision of the rag-picker. Think well of yourself . . . look on the sunny side of everything . . . talk health, happiness, and prosperity to every person you meet.

—Supreme Philosophy of Man

Most people are positive, will attempt to do the right thing, will treat others fairly, and will want to work together in harmony. It is critical that we keep this perspective to ensure we maintain a positive attitude. Yes, there are exceptions, but the exceptions should be addressed as isolated incidents rather than the norm. Similarly, never indict all for the actions of a few. There will be occasions when successive negative incidents will require us to have tremendous strength. It is important to remember that a negative approach affects our disposition, our attitude, and our performance. The positive approach allows us to maintain focus even when encountering adversity.

A man's life is what his thoughts make it.

—Marcus Aurelius (AD 121–180), Roman political leader

Our success is just as dependent upon our thoughts as our actions. We accomplish only what we believe we can. For this reason, it is important to visualize the attitude we are seeking and focus our thoughts on maintaining that mental attitude. Visualizing requires concentration, seeing the desired results, and keeping the image ever present. When we fixate on a mental image of the positive attitude we are seeking, we increase the energy and greatly enhance our determination. Visualization helps us maintain focus. If we are to succeed, we must maintain a positive attitude, continue to visualize success, and develop a strong work ethic.

In every organization and throughout life, there will be many individuals who influence us and our attitudes by their support, encouragement, or just their positive approach to life. As we receive this input or support, we should accept it graciously as a bonus. However, we must also recognize that developing and maintaining a positive attitude must be internally generated.

The Elevator Operator

Immediately after high school, I took time away from studies and worked for a copy center delivering photostatic copies. Because many of our clients were small local advertising agencies and centrally located, I delivered to the same building many different times during the day. One building, in particular, had an office adjacent to the lobby that was always occupied by an eccentric elderly lady. I later found out that she was the owner and had recently assumed the sole management role after the death of her husband. As time passed, she began speaking every time I entered the building and eventually initiated brief conversations. At the age of sixteen, my thoughts were focused on teenage issues, saving for college, and not on building relationships. However, I had been taught to always respect the elderly so I entertained her conversations.

Eventually I entered undergraduate school, focused on my studies, and thought nothing about my prior work experience. The following summer, it was difficult to find employment, so I began retracing steps, knocking on doors, and asking for work. When I approached the eccentric elderly lady, she thought for a moment and then said she could use an elevator operator. The building had two automatic elevators that had operated quite well for years without an operator. However, since it was a job offer, I did not ask why she wanted an operator for automatic elevators. Later, during a conversation she said, "I really didn't need an elevator operator, but you were always courteous and respectful." For two summers and most major holidays, I was an elevator operator for two automatic elevators. The job was instrumental in paying for two years of undergraduate studies and many other incidental expenses.

Lesson on Professionalism

Always carry yourself in a professional manner since you are marketing yourself all day, every day. The people you meet, and least expect, may hold the key to your future.

Of course, throughout life we will be confronted with many unpleasant circumstances both personally and professionally. Dolphins live in an environment with many predators, yet they maintain their positive attitude. Just as with dolphins, it is important that we maintain a positive attitude or approach at all times regardless of the circumstances or how difficult a situation may appear. Perceptions are our reality, and how we perceive issues, ideas, or assignments often defines our beliefs. If our perceptions are positive and our confidence intact, we maintain a positive attitude in everything we do. However, if our perceptions are negative, we bring this unhealthiness into our attitude and our approach to every encounter. We must find a way to maintain optimism, confidence, and passion for each assignment regardless of the perceived significance. By maintaining a positive attitude, similar to that demonstrated by dolphins, it instinctively affects our performance, outlook, enthusiasm, and the reception we receive from others. If we believe in ourselves, have prepared ourselves well, continue to maintain a positive attitude, and are committed to our goals, we will be well situated to reach our destination. Therefore, maintaining a positive attitude is essential for success.

The Terminated Employee

During my first supervisory position, I was forced to terminate an employee. Although I made the decision carefully and reluctantly, it was an easy decision since the employee was often absent from work with no valid excuse. Other employees were then required to perform his duties. In addition, since this was a service organization, his absence negatively affected the quality of service provided to customers. After many counseling sessions that failed to significantly change his attitude or reliability, I had to consider the tremendous implications his absence had on other employees and customers. I decided to terminate his employment and replaced him with a more reliable employee. He failed to accept responsibility for his actions or recognize that his performance caused the dismissal. He approached my manager without my knowledge and formally complained about his dismissal. His complaints were that he had been fired unjustly, I had deliberately singled him out for mistreatment, and my action was overzealous because of inexperience. Although I understood his request for reinstatement, the complaint was grossly inaccurate. It represented a personal attack on my supervisory skills. More importantly, it was an assault on my character and credibility. Even though this specific situation was resolved to my satisfaction and the employee was not rehired, the incident taught me some critical lessons very early in my career.

Lesson: Maintain A Positive Attitude

Make the difficult decisions, do what is right, defend your position, keep a positive attitude, avoid retaliating, and do not personalize issues. In spite of personal attacks, you must continue to maintain a positive attitude about people.

Attitudes can be negatively affected by

- Changes in the organizational structure;

- Changes in leadership;

- Changes to improve customer responsiveness;

- Organizational competitiveness.

With a positive attitude, these changes are accepted as environmental, and the appropriate adjustments are made. However, for many, there is a tendency to be inflexible and resist change. Yes, there are explanations for the resistance such as the following:

- **Habit**—We are comfortable with the status quo; change is difficult.

- **Fear**—We are unwilling to face the unknown.

- **Advice**—Others suggest the resistance often for their personal benefit.

- **Personal**—Change affects our personal status.

In spite of these reasons, recognize that change is inevitable. The level of our resistance, if persistent, will result in our being labeled as not being a team player. This label will impact future organizational advancement. However, let me quickly add that resistance, when there are ethical issues, is quite appropriate.

We should always follow the example of dolphins and avoid allowing negativism to affect our attitudes. Unfortunately, there are individuals or groups within most organizations who spread negative energy that is organizationally directed, personally directed, and sometimes just misdirected. Because there are negative forces at play, it is our responsibility to filter out and reject the negative influences. Many of those advancing the negative energy can be classified as (1) promoters of negativism, (2) gossipmongers, and (3) backstabbers.

❖ **Promoters of Negativism**—In most organizations, there are individuals or groups of individuals who criticize every action or decision. Their approach is to consistently search for a negative or create one in every decision or event affecting the organization. As a result, they are often negative or at best pessimistic and, whether knowingly or unknowingly, spread this negativism throughout the organization. Their negativism, if left unchecked, often acts as a cancer that permeates the entire organization. This negativism adversely affects the attitude of employees and subsequently their performance. Participating or allowing ourselves to be involved in these negative discussions or perceptions adversely impacts attitude and distracts focus away from our goals. We should never allow ourselves to be associated with these negative thoughts or spend time with these negative people. Their messages are contagious, and they will eventually adversely impact our perceptions, thoughts, and energy. Their messages accomplish nothing, destroy morale, negatively affect performance, and cause us to spend unnecessary energy that could be focused more positively.

❖ **Gossipmongers**—In most organizations, there are individuals who spend an enormous amount of their time spreading information about the organization and individuals within the organization. The information is often negative, misleading, demeaning, inaccurate, and valueless to the organization and the individual. In fact, this gossip has no intrinsic value to anyone. We should avoid association with the gossipmongers and their information flow in spite of how inviting the information may sound. Associating with or becoming involved with these groups has four distinctively negative implications:

- The integrity of the individuals participating in the gossiping is often questionable, especially if the validity of the information is not ironclad.

- By associating with the information, especially if it has negative implications, we adversely affect others' careers and livelihoods.

- The information can often adversely affect our attitudes, which may lead to personal performance issues.

- We are judged by the company we keep. Decision makers often believe that the individuals involved are more interested in gossiping than performing. This perception can have negative implications for our job progression.

For these reasons, if we avoid involvement or association with gossipmongers as well as the information flowing from these individuals, we will improve our attitude. It will also allow us to continue focusing on goals.

Let me distinguish between gossip and important information received from others within the organization. There is an informal communication channel in most organizations that is both necessary and effective. The informal channel is often established, efficient, and much more current than the formal communication channel. It is from these sources that we learn valuable information about the organization, its customs, and practices. We must distinguish between information delivered by gossipmongers and information from established but informal sources. One of the major distinctions is that information from the gossipmongers is often negative while information from the informal channels is factual and widely discussed.

❖ **Backstabbers**—Unfortunately, not all of our coworkers are always supportive. There are individuals who enjoy spreading falsehoods or who attempt to put roadblocks in our paths. Backstabbing is the term used to describe these negative actions. Backstabbers are the individuals perpetrating these actions. Their actions affect us personally since the acts are vicious, perpetrated knowingly, and are designed with negative intentions. They backstab because of their insecurity or often just to derail our progress. Should we be the recipient of the backstabber's act, we clearly must address the incident and the individual directly. However, it is most important that we maintain professionalism at all times and never allow ourselves to fall into the trap of seeking revenge for their actions.

We must also personally avoid involvement or perpetuating these actions by backstabbing others. The participants not only lack integrity, but the cost to those involved can be devastating. However, we should always be aware that backstabbers exist in most organizations. Avoid involvement, address the action perpetrated against you, and stay above the fray since no one wins in any form of backstabbing.

My Trusted Senior Executive

During one's career, there are always experiences, both positive and negative, that defy logic and leave a lasting impression. One of my more memorable experiences occurred relatively late in my career. Without my knowledge, one of the senior executives who reported to me, whom I trusted, requested and obtained a private meeting with the chief executive of the organization. His sole purpose was to lodge a personal complaint about me to the highest level in the organization. Even today, I am not entirely sure of the full content of the discussion. However, the essence of his complaint was that my management style was stifling his creativity and his progressive ideas were being rejected outright or, at best, receiving minimal consideration. His meeting with the chief executive followed a private discussion I had with him on his lack of involvement. We also discussed ways he could be more productive. During our discussion, he acknowledged that he had been disconnected. He also identified numerous reasons for his lack of productivity. I perceived the meeting as a way to improve his performance and benefit the organization. He obviously viewed it as a threat. I learned of their private meeting only by chance. During my subsequent regularly scheduled meeting with the chief executive, he asked a very casual question, "How are you and . . . working together as a team?" After many years of experience, I was aware that this question was not just a casual inquiry. As our discussion progressed, the chief executive reluctantly revealed that the senior executive had requested the private meeting with him and lodged the personal complaint.

My belief was that, at best, the senior executive's comments were designed to create a positive impression with the chief executive. At worst, they were designed to create doubt about my management style at the highest level of the organization. Regardless of his rationale, I found this episode difficult to accept. I was surprised by, did not expect, nor was I prepared for his actions. This episode reconfirmed that backstabbing is alive, well, and active at all levels in organizations.

During our subsequent, very candid discussion, the senior executive reluctantly acknowledged the meeting. He revealed some details of the discussion, attempted to explain his rationale, and tried to appear contrite. It was the epitome of betrayal or backstabbing at the highest possible level. This action was also a major miscalculation on his part since it resulted in a complete loss of trust, displayed his lack of integrity, and rendered him ineffective. More importantly, it diminished his value to the organization and resulted in his subsequent departure.

Lesson on Attitude

Even though there are individuals who will perpetrate negative actions, maintain your integrity and recognize that these actions are individual acts. Do not generalize. Instead, focus your response on that individual act only. This approach will enable you to maintain a positive attitude about people even during the adversity.

It is not uncommon to underestimate the degree to which attitude impacts all of our other activities. Because it affects our demeanor, outlook, and performance, it is imperative that we remain positive at all times. This positive approach, regardless of the environment, is evident in the attitude of dolphins. They do not allow negative external influences to affect their positive nature. Although there are some people who will attempt to negatively affect our attitude, it is essential that we maintain our integrity and never allow their actions to affect us. If we accept negative external influences, we, in effect, transfer our power and the level of our performance to others.

They can because they think they can.

—Virgil (70–19 BC), Roman poet and writer

Chapter Seven

Networks— The Hornbill and the Mongoose

Skill is fine, and genius is splendid, but the right contacts are more valuable than either.

—Sir Archibald McIndoe (1900–1960), New Zealand plastic surgeon

PRINCIPLE SEVEN

Foster Relationships to Enhance Recognition, Ensure Development, Create Opportunities, and Promote Success.

Networking of the Hornbill and the Mongoose

There are many examples of networking between birds during their nesting and feeding. There are also many examples of other animals networking in their environment. However, the networking between the African hornbill (bird) and the dwarf mongoose (mammal) is relatively unique. On hunting trips, the mongoose leads the way with his head down, flushing out insects and small reptiles that the hornbill uses for food. The hornbill, with his head up, is very vigilant in warning the mongoose of impending danger. The hornbill will visit the sleeping site of the mongoose and give a loud call to signal its readiness to begin the day. If late, the mongoose will wait for its arrival. Both the bird and the mammal work together, or network, to accomplish their individual objectives.

Lesson Inspired by Nature

You should be just as diligent as the hornbill and the mongoose: ignore individual differences and build relationships, or networks, to accomplish your personal goals.

The most important single ingredient in the formula of success is knowing how to get along with people.

—Theodore Roosevelt (1858–1919), US president and politician

Strong Networks

A network is an informal relationship that is often loosely formed for the purpose of assisting in or enhancing a specific goal, interest, or career. It is a community of individuals with disparate backgrounds and interests that, taken together, work toward a common goal. Networking, in this context, requires forming relationships and managing them in a manner that improves our visibility and progress in an organization. Even though networking involves developing relationships with the expectation of personally benefiting, we should never perceive it as using people. It is quite useful, expected, practiced, and uniformly accepted in professional organizations. In many cases, just as with the hornbill and the mongoose, there are mutual benefits resulting from the networks.

There are many talented individuals who perform their jobs very well, but they will not all progress at the same pace because of real or perceived differences. Even if there are few significant performance differences, the advancement is often awarded to the individual who has better connections or is better known by the cadre of decision makers. For this reason, it is important to always have advocates in that cadre of decision makers. It has been reported that over 50 percent of external jobs are filled based on contacts developed through networks. While the percentage can be debated, we will agree that many decisions are made based on prior contacts. Networking provides that extra edge or the enhancement that moves us ahead of our contemporaries. How well we develop our networks may well determine our overall success.

Networking is universal and needed in many aspects of our lives and careers. We noted the universality of it with the hornbill and the mongoose. Networking is also very beneficial for many external career changes, business involvement, and personal promotions. However, in this context, we will focus only on that networking necessary for advancement in our current organizations.

> **No matter how much work a man can do, no matter how engaging his personality may be, he will not advance far in business if he cannot work through others.**
>
> —John Craig

Networks will never replace stellar performance since there are few people who will act as an advocate for us unless they are convinced we are worthy of their support. Without excellent performance, we will find it extremely difficult to establish networks that will promote advancement within the organization. Advocates must be convinced that if they promote our advancement, we will be able to perform effectively. If individuals advocate for us and we do not perform, it damages their credibility. That is why performance is a prerequisite for successful network development.

Networking Without Performance

Jeff worked within my organization and spent a considerable amount of time networking with others. He knew many people within the organization and spent considerable time discussing his goals and ambition with them. His networking extended to all levels of the organization including many within the management cadre as well members of the maintenance and service groups. In effect, Jeff was very effective in promoting himself in circles that he thought would assist in his career development. He dressed well, was professional, handsome, articulate, and well liked by most people with whom he associated. Unfortunately, he failed to make a similar investment in his personal preparation and performance. My advice and counsel was not enough encouragement to cause him to focus on his performance. Because of his focus on networking, he did not receive consideration for many opportunities simply because he failed to be as committed to his performance as to his network development. Many potential advocates, myself included, were reluctant to promote his advancement because we were concerned that his performance would be unacceptable.

> ## Lesson: Networking with Performance
> Networking is critical for your continued advancement within an organization. However, to advance in your career, you cannot rely solely on networking. You must have a similar focus on preparation and performance.

Networking is a process that we must own and view as a significant part of our performance. We should never assume that our job performance alone will result in our being adopted by a mentor or a cadre of decision makers.

Network development requires hard work and, particularly, the mastering of soft skills or people skills. Necessary skills are diplomacy, empathy, trust, awareness, flexibility, adaptability, self-control, and sociability. We must demonstrate that we can be more than just a technical performer. It requires a mastering of the many skills discussed throughout the chapters of this book. In effect, we must be prepared with all of the skills to meet the challenges that may confront us. These same skills are necessary not only for networking but for many other activities in our personal and professional lives. Many of these networking skills are learned over time and honed through continuous use.

> **The greatest ability in business is to get along with others and influence their actions. A chip on the shoulder is too heavy a piece of baggage to carry through life.**
>
> —John Hancock (1737–1793), US governor and statesman

In spite of the many statements on the objectivity of the process, many personnel selections are made based solely on the comfort level of the person making the selection. Either consciously or subconsciously there has been a historic tendency to use similarities as a major decision factor. In many organizations, this tendency accounts for the significant disparity in representation of women and individuals with different ethnic backgrounds. In spite of this sobering reality, it is still important to develop networks and have them operating effectively. Without the networks, we reduce the likelihood of actually being considered for potential advancement.

The term networks has been used deliberately since more than one network is required. Networks are necessary, not only to ensure we reach our goals, but to ensure that we receive input and guidance from many sources. Our cadre of networks should include (1) internal decision-makers' network, (2) external consultative network, (3) employee network, and (4) social network.

❖ **Internal Decision-Makers' Network**—It is important to know who the decision makers are in the organization and to develop a network that includes some of these decision makers. This network is essential to support our organizational advancement. It is significant since the decision makers are in positions to advocate for us at times when it is impossible to advocate for ourselves. We have often heard that to advance in organizations we must identify a mentor and be pulled or pushed upward in the organization. There have been many success stories utilizing mentoring, and many other people will benefit from the process. However, in today's environment, it is much more risky to limit ourselves to this approach. The one individual that we identify as our mentor may quickly lose favor in the organization and leave us without an anchor. Additionally, the risk of losing our advocate has increased because of the significant movement of individuals between organizations. With the increase in mergers, divestments, and other organizational changes, there is now significantly less stability in the executive pool than there was in the past. For these reasons, it is more desirable to utilize a network of decision makers who have our interest and advancement as a priority. The likelihood that all members of the network will simultaneously lose favor or transfer out of the organization is significantly less likely. The major concern is that by limiting ourselves and putting all of our hope in one senior official, our advancement will be aligned with his or her advancement and stability.

The Prestigious Position

During my many years in organizations, I had the opportunity to provide advice and counsel to a number of individuals. Some accepted my advice while others rejected it outright. One such case was an individual whom I was instrumental in bringing into the organization. Although he had prepared himself well technically, he never seemed to overwhelm people with his performance. We often discussed ways to improve his performance and networking within the organization. The techniques discussed were beneficial since he was beginning to gain recognition and favor. He soon asked my advice on campaigning for an external, non-paying, non-career-related officer position in a national organization. Although the prestige would have been tremendous, my strong advice was to delay such an effort. I advised him to first focus on internal networking. Obviously, the potential prestige was too much of a temptation. He campaigned for the position. The result was that he failed in his external bid and his internal performance deteriorated. Eventually, he resigned from the organization, defeated on both accounts.

Lesson: Setting Priorities

Although external recognition and prestige are important, they should not take priority over your internal networking and performance. Even if you gain the external prestige but fail in your performance, you have still lost.

❖ **External Consultative Network**—It is also necessary to develop a network outside of the organization's environment. Remember how the hornbill and the mongoose reached outside of their species and developed a network? We can use our external consultative network for private consultation. This network should include contemporaries in different organizations who have relatively similar experiences. The similar experiences will enhance the relationship and make for the following:

- A more meaningful dialogue
- A more dynamic exchange of ideas
- A more involved discussion of strategy
- More input on pending issues

At the very least, this network should include individuals who have insight into the internal operations of organizations. Because of their experience, they can provide feedback on issues. It should definitely include individuals with whom we can speak confidentially since it is inevitable we will encounter issues that we are uncomfortable discussing with others in our organization. The purpose of the network should not be to always get resolution on an issue. Instead, it should provide the opportunity to openly discuss issues and gain valuable input.

Networking Support That Matters

I was extremely fortunate to be involved with an organization that included many successful individuals employed by local corporate organizations. We met frequently with the primary purpose of learning and supporting each other. These sessions allowed for an open exchange of ideas, discussions of similar issues, and the opportunity to learn from others. The dialogues were powerful and extremely beneficial because of similarities in backgrounds and experiences. These sessions also provided the platform for private discussions with selected participants. The private sessions enabled me to gain additional input on issues that I could not openly discuss in my organization or with the entire external group. However, because the issues were of significance and a major personal concern, the dialogues were extremely beneficial. This external consultative network was enormously helpful to me. The members provided the type of insight and support that was unavailable in my organization.

> ## Lesson: External Contacts
> It does not matter the level of preparation, the number of networks, or the amount of other support; you should always maintain external contacts with whom you can consult in confidence. If members of the network are both knowledgeable and supportive, they will provide invaluable input and improve the quality of your performance and decision making.

❖ **Employee Network**—Often, we overlook or minimize the significance of developing an employee network because we often perceive this group as powerless. On the contrary, this network is essential and can play a vital role for us in the organization. The employee network should include peers, administrative and support staff, and others with primary roles in the organization. These individuals have access to key individuals and useful information that can be critical in helping us stay aware of organizational developments. This is not suggesting that we use them to reveal sensitive information since divulging that type of information could become an integrity issue. However, the information they provide will enable us to position ourselves for key assignments or other significant activities. There is a distinct difference between employee networks and just gossiping. Clearly, my intent here is not to imply that we become involved with office gossip. In fact, we should avoid those relationships just as we would the plague. Negative comments are often attributed to gossipmongers, and this association could be detrimental to careers. What I am suggesting is that we establish and maintain a network of individuals who have access to invaluable factual information. This network can be extremely beneficial to us in the organization.

An Inconsistent Performance Review

On a major assignment, I received a stellar oral and written performance evaluation from a senior executive. As a result of this evaluation, I was elated with my accomplishment, my progress in the organization, and the organization's perception of my performance. As a continuation of the performance review process, the human resources department and senior executives held a follow-up meeting to rank key professionals. Needless to say, I was very comfortable with the written input and believed that I would rank very well among my contemporaries. Fortunately, the administrative support individual recording this meeting was part of my employee network. Later, she informed me privately of some negative personal comments made by the same senior executive who had given me the stellar performance review. I was glad that she had the courage to advise me of the inconsistent comments. After absorbing the shock and disbelief, I had several dialogues with executives in my decision-makers' network. They confirmed that negative comments were made but that the comments were challenged since they differed substantially from the written input. Yes, I was able to address this inconsistency and not reveal the source of the information. However, I would not have received the feedback without my employee network. The verbal comments might not have been challenged without my internal decision-makers' network. The results could have been very detrimental to my long-term career without the support from my networks.

Lesson: Importance of Networks

Networks are critical and should not be limited to just those individuals above you on the company's organization chart. You must develop networks at all levels of the organization to gain invaluable information that will promote your career success.

❖ **Social Network**—While any discussion on social networks in a general discussion of organizations is somewhat unique, it is nevertheless an important aspect of our career development. When using the term "social network," we are not suggesting that we develop this network within our organization. Rather, it is suggesting that we maintain an external social network because of its organizational performance implications. Social networks add balance to life; they provide an outlet, a diversion, an opportunity to unwind, and the avenue for reenergizing ourselves. This diversion is vital for our continued success. Even though we may not utilize all of our social networks frequently, it is comforting just knowing they are available.

The Need for a Social Network

I spent a few years in a foreign country working in a senior position of a worldwide organization. While the day-to-day job requirements were easily manageable, the lack of a social network was perhaps the most difficult adjustment for me and my family. Without this network, the opportunity for unwinding or maintaining balance in my life made job performance much more difficult. Shortly after the relocation, we attempted to replace the network with other activities. However, these activities did not provide the necessary social contact. Since we are social beings, activities can not replace personal contacts. Although we eventually began to establish a cadre of friends and acquaintances, this experience reinforced my strong belief that we can not limit ourselves to professional, external, or outside interests. We must also have social networks to effectively face the organizational challenges. Yes, these networks can be built; however, building requires time and significant effort, especially when there are cultural barriers involved. We cannot hope to continuously perform well without other sources of outlet external to the job. The saying "All work and no play makes Jack a dull boy" definitely has merit.

> ## Lesson: Avoid Isolation
>
> You cannot perform at your best if you are isolated. Develop social contacts or sources of outlet to maintain balance in life and improve the quality of your performance.

❖ **Mentor**—Some years ago, it was commonplace to advise professional employees to choose a mentor in the organization. It was also expected that organization officials would mentor at least one employee. It was one of the predominant methods used to develop employees and prepare them for future leadership positions. However, individuals are now spending less time in a single organization because of structural changes and many other factors. There is a significant increase in job changes and less of the blind loyalty to professional organizations that was prevalent years ago. With the increased personnel movement, seeking a single mentor is less appealing. Let me quickly add, I am not implying that organizations no longer embrace the mentoring concept. Many organizations still utilize mentorship as part of their management development plan and utilize it very effectively. However, the fact that I discuss mentoring after the decision-makers' network is deliberate and is done for several reasons:

- While it is important to have a mentor, having only one advocate leaves us attached to only one individual. Even though that one mentor may be the only advocate needed, frequently, individuals lose their mentors because of organizational changes, and they subsequently flounder until they build new relationships.

- Often, the mentor is either not readily available or cannot effectively advocate for us. This unavailability is a result of the increase in the size of organizations, the worldwide movement of personnel, or the departure externally of many individuals. If the advocate is unavailable, we must start the process of building another mentor relationship from the beginning. Even though we may have invested considerable time building the relationship and gaining the admiration and trust of the mentor, that time is lost.

This is not to suggest that if a mentor is available we should refuse his or her support. Instead, in addition to the mentor, we should continue to cultivate networks. Yes, mentorship has many positive implications, and there are many related success stories. However, developing relationships with a cadre of decision makers will be beneficial when faced with many of today's adverse organizational or personnel issues.

A Mentor Lost

My organization did not have a formal mentorship program as part of its professional development. However, after establishing myself and demonstrating strong work standards, I identified a mentor and developed an extremely comfortable relationship. From a personal perspective, I was comfortable knowing that he was a strong advocate for me. Our bond was strong because he was very confident that my performance was solid, I had potential for additional responsibilities, and I would live up to the trust that he placed in me. While this mentor relationship lasted for some years and was very beneficial, suddenly, as part of an organizational downsizing, he, along with many others, was offered early retirement. His departure left me without an effective advocate and forced me to find others to serve the same role. I then began developing that network of decision makers who eventually became my advocates. Yes, there was time lost in the process. However, because of the tremendous organizational upheaval, the process was minimized. Many of my peers faced the same fate. Since there were many new officials with decision-making responsibility, I was able to regroup, build a network of decision makers, and continue my progress within the organization. Over the years, many faces changed because of subsequent organizational changes, acquisitions, and divestitures. Because of the many changes, this network of decision makers became even more critical.

Lesson: Relationships

Mentors can be extremely important for career advancement, but you should also develop other relationships. The diversification will enable you to avoid being adversely affected by organizational turmoil or personnel changes.

Tim's Misguided Mentorship

The purpose of mentorship is to provide objective advice, counsel, and support to an individual for the purpose of improving career advancement. It is not to duplicate the leadership style of the mentor. Tim, an extremely talented colleague of mine, was progressing well in the organization. He decided to adopt the brash, insensitive, and obnoxious style of his mentor. The negative style was extremely degrading to employees and caused Tim to develop many enemies. Tim was tolerated in the organization because of the tacit support of his mentor. The mentor had survived, progressed, and was a member of the senior management team in spite of his style. However, the mentor left the organization for another opportunity and left Tim without a mentor, with many enemies, and with a style that was unacceptable to the organization. Needless to say, within a matter of months Tim was asked, unceremoniously, to leave the organization. I am not sure if Tim developed his style based on input from his mentor or if it was inherent. His obnoxious style was not evident during a previous three-year period when he worked for me. Regardless, his lost mentor and negative leadership style caused his failure in the organization.

Lesson: Build Healthy Relationships

Accept advice and counsel from mentors graciously, but understand that you must be able to survive without the mentor's support. Build healthy relationships with others throughout the organization to aid in your development, advocate for your advancement, and assist in the pursuit of your goals.

❖ **Mentoring Others**—As we progress in an organization, we should create opportunities to mentor other aspiring individuals. There are many very capable individuals looking for that special opportunity or seeking the advice and encouragement that will assist them in their organizational advancement. We should avoid ignoring them or failing to share experiences. By reaching out to others, we become teachers, but more importantly, we are also students who learn and benefit from the experience.

In every environment, networking is critical to ensure personal goals are accomplished. The networking of the hornbill and the mongoose provides evidence that networking is utilized effectively in many environments. My personal experiences demonstrate the importance networking played in my career development. Others have been just as successful utilizing networks to promote their career development. Because of the proven success, we should all develop internal decision-makers', external consultative, employee, and social networks to promote our careers and maintain balance in our lives.

If we have the mistaken idea that, in order to be an adult and mature, we need to go it alone, we should remember that even the most successful and talented athletes have coaches who guide, encourage, and instruct them. We need coaches too. It is important we learn from the examples of others who have successfully been down the road we are traveling.

—Sue Patton Thoele, US author,
speaker, and marriage and family therapist

Chapter Eight

Teamwork and Geese

Individual commitment to a group effort—that is
what makes a team work, a company work, a society
work, a civilization work.

—Vince Lombardi (1913–1970),
Hall of Fame football coach, Green Bay Packers

PRINCIPLE EIGHT

Recognize That Teamwork Is Essential to Accomplish Personal, Professional, and Organizational Goals.

Teamwork of Geese

The seasonal migration of geese and the V formation they use in flight is a tremendous study in teamwork:

- The formation adds uplift, reduces resistance, and increases the flying range of the entire flock.

- When the lead goose tires, it rotates back in the formation and another team member takes the lead.

- The entire flock constantly honks encouragement to maintain speed.

- If a goose is injured, several others drop out of formation to assist or protect the injured until it is able to fly again or dies. At that time, they may rejoin their original flock or another.

These geese clearly display individual effort, but they utilize the team approach to efficiently migrate to distant locations.

Lesson Inspired by Nature

If geese can utilize such tremendous teamwork to accomplish their individual objectives, then surely we should do no less.

The Stone Cutters

There is an old story from an unknown author about two stonecutters busy at work. When they were asked what they were doing, the first replied, "I am cutting the stones into blocks." The second answered, "I am on a team, building a cathedral." The question we must constantly ask ourselves is, are we individual stonecutters or are we team players working toward the team's goals?

Lesson: Team Concept

Regardless of the task, remember that you are performing as part of a larger team. Make sure that your role is performed effectively for both personal and organizational success.

A Team Concept

Teamwork is a cooperative or a collaborative effort by individuals to accomplish a specific task. The team is made up of a group of individuals working toward a mutually dependent common objective. Teamwork requires the ability to build alliances and direct individual accomplishments toward organizational objectives. Every individual, regardless of his or her organization, current position, or long-term goals, must demonstrate the ability to perform as a valuable member of a team to achieve success.

An Unreliable Team Member

I was newly assigned to a first-line management position in an accounting department. We were required to work closely with another accounting group to obtain critical cost information prior to completing our tasks. The information was to be written, approved, and submitted by a predetermined date. Once, the manager of that department indicated that even though his group had not finalized the information in the agreed time, he would verbally provide the information and submit the formal documents later. In effect, his organization had failed to complete their tasks in a timely manner. In my eagerness to be seen as a team player, I accepted the information verbally and proceeded to meet my established deadline. Several days later, it was disclosed that the information he provided was grossly in error. The manager had either deliberately or inadvertently misled me and left me exposed to senior management. Needless to say, I was reprimanded for my failure to adequately verify and document the information I had presented. My eagerness to be seen as a team player resulted in my overlooking a major organizational requirement.

Lesson: Limitation on Team Play

Although team play is critical, never assume responsibility for other team members' failures. Accept responsibility for your shortcomings, but do not automatically assume that all team members are capable, reliable, and worthy of your trust.

Maintaining strong, effective, and efficient operating teams is essential for the survival of most organizations. We noted how geese maintain highly functioning teams to accomplish personal gain and positive results for the flock. Similarly, organizations expect every employee to be a member of a highly functioning team. Although many teams form, operate, and disband, they can be included in one of the following three categories:

❖ **Work Teams**—This is the most common team and the one in which most employees will perform their daily tasks. These teams are ongoing and required to deliver the mission or the objectives of the workgroup.

❖ **Cross-Functional Teams**—These teams include a cadre of individuals from different workgroups assigned to a project to accomplish a specific goal. The individual members may not have shared goals, but their combined efforts provide the desired results.

❖ **Action Teams**—These groups are organized to resolve a specific problem. They have a common objective, but once the specific problem is resolved and the objective accomplished, the team is disbanded.

The degree to which these teams build alliances, collaborate, and accomplish objectives determines the organization's effectiveness.

In spite of the attempt to ensure the effectiveness of teams, many fail. Although considerable time is spent after the fact analyzing the reasons for failure, most will fall into one of three basic categories:

❖ **Definitions**—The goals or objectives of the team are not clearly defined and understood by team members well enough to ensure there is consistent team focus. Additionally, the individual roles and responsibilities are not well understood by team members to ensure they know what they are being asked to do. Unless definitions are clear, the team becomes dysfunctional and fails to accomplish the identified objectives.

❖ **Leadership**—Every team requires effective leadership to ensure that the team members are working toward the common goal. The leader must maintain focus on the goals and be able to coordinate the individual efforts, adjust direction, change objectives, provide motivation, and refocus the team to ensure the objectives are accomplished. To be effective, the leader must be decisive, timely, and provide feedback to individual members. Failure in any of these areas can cause the team to be ineffective.

❖ **Team Members**—The individual performance of team members working toward a common goal is critical for the success of a team. The teams will not be effective if there are significant personality conflicts, private agendas, or a lack of trust between members. These factors inhibit openness, the free flow of information, and the sharing of ideas, which are all critical for team success.

As a team performer, we must be clear on the team objectives and our roles and responsibilities in accomplishing those objectives. Additionally, our effort must be directed toward being an effective, reliable, and trusted team member. Regardless of whether we are in the position of establishing, leading, or performing on teams, we must focus on ways to avoid team failures.

An Ineffective Team

On a major assignment, I was faced with a dysfunctional team. The department was divided into two separate groups:

- A centralized group responsible for policy development and certain organization-wide projects.

- A large decentralized group responsible for day-to-day service delivery to a large customer base.

It was impossible for the team to be effective without a close working relationship. However, they did not respect each other, were extremely inefficient, and failed to communicate effectively. Their dysfunctional relationship had been allowed to continue under the leadership of a grandfatherly figure until his retirement.

I initially tried some soft approaches to resolve the issues causing the problems within the dysfunctional team:

- Team meetings to begin a dialogue with the hopes of building bridges.

- Facilitated meetings to identify the problems causing the dysfunction.

- Joint objectives to encourage working together.

Unfortunately, the result of this soft approach was more finger-pointing with no substantial increase in the team's effectiveness. They had developed a level of comfort with the status quo.

The next approach was to reorganize the department, integrate the groups, identify some new leaders, and develop specific individual performance objectives for the key members. This organizational upheaval had substantial risks:

- It had the potential for disrupting service delivery.

- It placed employees in positions with which they were not familiar.

- It removed a level of comfort for many employees, which made the change unpopular.

- It placed less experienced employees in leadership roles.

Although there were some initial performance issues, some disgruntled employees, and some grievances filed, the reorganization proved to be effective in improving team performance.

Lesson: Team Effectiveness

The effectiveness of a team is much more important than the comfort of the individual members. Your unique expertise is not enough to overcome ineffective teamwork. Maintain strong team performance or you risk being summarily replaced.

If a team is to reach its potential, each player must be willing to subordinate his personal goals to the good of the team.

—Bud Wilkinson (1916–1994),
professional football coach, St. Louis Cardinals

Sometimes we must sacrifice individual accomplishments or personal gain for the overall benefit of the team. While sacrifice is normal, expected, and uniformly accepted, we must ensure that our entire career is not just sacrificing with little personal gain or recognition. Even though there is no "I" in "team," there will be ample opportunity to express individualism while performing under the team concept. Because of the unavoidability of teamwork, we must find a way and demonstrate the ability to work for others' interests while maintaining focus on individual or personal goals.

Since the organization's success is dependent upon the effectiveness of teams, being a team player and contributing to that team is critical for individual success. There are ten personal qualities that must be mastered to effectively perform the team role (1) communication, (2) competence, (3) collaboration, (4) professionalism, (5) relationship building, (6) commitment, (7) dependability, (8) flexibility, (9) inclusiveness, and (10) support.

❖ **Communication**—Effective communication is a key ingredient that must be mastered to enable the efficient operation of a team. Communication in a team environment requires listening, keeping others aware of project status, and soliciting assistance. These are all necessary to ensure tasks are performed efficiently, effectively, and in a timely manner. In effect, information must flow openly, freely, uninhibited, uninterrupted, and without judgment to ensure input from all team members. Effective communication builds more trusting relationships within the team, which encourages all members to become more actively involved.

❖ **Competence**—There is an underlying expectation that every team member will be competent and be able to perform their roles and responsibilities. It requires both a physical and mental commitment to the pursuit of excellence. The role assigned requires consistency in our approach, actions, and delivery. Although these expectations may never be openly discussed by team members, be aware that a lack of adequate preparation will result in personal failure. Our ability to efficiently perform the assigned tasks is constantly being observed. Anything short of adequate preparation and total commitment to the task is a disservice to the organization, the team, and eventually, to the individual.

❖ **Collaboration**—Sharing information with other team members is essential to ensure that the team can effectively perform its tasks. If we are part of a team, all team members working toward a common objective, and our roles are essential, then the free flow of information is crucial to achieve team success. Hoarding information that would enhance team performance to demonstrate individualism or to magnify our contributions is not an acceptable practice. Similarly, refusing to share ideas that could positively improve team performance is just as unacceptable. Withholding information, refusing to participate, and practicing individualism are definitely quick ways to shorten a career. Teamwork requires sharing thoughts and ideas openly and listening to input from other team members. Even though there may be diametrically opposing views within the team, it is critical to listen, be open, and maintain a cordial relationship.

Teamwork requires that everyone's efforts flow in a single direction. Feelings of significance happen when a team's energy takes on a life of its own.

—Pat Riley, professional basketball coach, Miami Heat

❖ **Professionalism**—We must maintain a high level of professionalism at all times. It is through professionalism that we demonstrate confidence, begin to build trust, and develop a positive relationship with other team members. Actions, either positive or negative, reflect on the individual and the team. Professionalism improves personal and team image and increases the team's effectiveness. Demonstrating integrity, showing respect, and exhibiting courtesy to other members promotes cooperation on other significant issues. Professionalism enables the team to function much more effectively. More importantly, it improves our status on the team and in the organization.

❖ **Relationship Building**—To be an effective team player, relationships must be maintained at all times. Teams will not be effective simply by assigning individuals to work together. They are more than just a collection of individuals performing similar tasks. Just as we noted with geese, teams are groups built on relationships, performing individual roles, and working for common objectives. Individual members must be conscious of the common objective and work to develop relationships in the team. This requires being sensitive to other team members' needs and respecting them as individuals. Relationship building requires a willingness to accept ideas from others without being judgmental. It requires just getting along with other team members. We have all heard of sports teams that are extremely talented but continuously perform poorly and never live up to the team's potential. So it is in professional organizations. Talent alone will not necessarily result in an efficient team; relationships built on trust are necessary to be effective.

All your strength is in union, all your danger is in discord.

—Henry Wadsworth Longfellow (1807–1882), US poet and writer

- ❖ **Commitment**—To be an effective team member requires a commitment to the team's mission and goals. Like the wild geese, individual performance is improved when working on activities that enable a level of comfort, provide a sense of accomplishment, and add value to the team. These factors enable us to be more focused and involved with team activities. Likewise, it is impossible to perform effectively in an environment when we are not committed or when we are constantly questioning the team's goals, objectives, direction, or even our contribution. Without commitment, we are less focused, individual effort is hindered, performance is more difficult, and our contribution to the team suffers.

- ❖ **Dependability**—Again, like the wild geese, in a team environment, we must demonstrate a sense of responsibility and demonstrate that individual tasks will be completed timely and competently. Just as the wild geese depend on each other to maintain the formation of the flock, others will depend on us to perform our responsibilities.

Other team members must be comfortable and know that we are dependable and will take responsibility for our actions. They must also be able to depend on our sincerity, openness, thoroughness, and willingness to be supportive of the team.

Team Management Skills Tested

One of my most difficult assignments during my many years in organizations was coordinating the study of a major corporate-wide project. Because of a corporate reorganization, the project was undertaken to improve the efficiency of the organization. It was made difficult because of the following:

- A need for cooperation from many different work groups with different interests.

- The difficulty of the project. There were no prototypes to serve as a guide.

- Not having a dedicated team devoted full time to the project. Members were assigned temporarily from the participating groups to complete an assigned task.

- Inadequate funding for the project. We needed to prove the viability of the project to justify the funding.

- A historical lack of trust between the groups made working together difficult.

- Information and expertise were required from each group to be successful.

- The project results, if implemented, would negatively affect some of the groups involved in the study.

- Management responsibility for the participating groups was dispersed throughout the organization. Therefore, I did not have total authority with my position and could not always remove unproductive participants.

Although there were many significant barriers, the first to address was the lack of trust. Overcoming this barrier was necessary to build a sense of teamwork within the group.

I hired an independent group to anonymously survey members of the different groups to determine the issues causing the conflict. With the information gathered, I met jointly, in open session, to discuss ways of addressing the myriad of concerns. The purpose was to openly discuss concerns, clear the air of past differences, and move forward as a more cohesive team. Throughout the entire project, every coaching, cajoling, pleading, encouraging, networking, and relationship skill imaginable was required to keep the project moving forward.

We completed the assigned task and identified the organizational needs. However, we were unable to identify a vendor that could deliver our project requirements with any degree of certainty. Much of the success of the project was attributed to the trust that the team members had in me rather than a trusting relationship with other members of the team.

Lesson: Practice Skills

Leadership, teamwork, networking, and relationship-building skills are essential for your success. Develop these skills early and practice them continuously to ensure they are honed and can be utilized effectively when needed.

❖ **Flexibility**—We do not operate in a static environment. Instead, we are constantly faced with changing circumstances that often impact the team's direction, objectives, requirements, or even our personal involvement. We must be willing, able, and flexible enough to adapt to these changes if we are to be effective and contributing members of the team. Because of the frequency and significance of these ongoing changes, inflexibility will negatively impact our personal performance and the team's results.

❖ **Inclusiveness**—In order for teams to be effective, each member must be involved and perform tasks for the benefit of the group. We should make a concerted effort to ensure others are included in the team's activities. This requires involving them in our team actions to obtain additional insight, opinions, and input. It requires our providing similar input into the activities of other team members. Because of individual differences, unique thought patterns, environmental impact, or specialized training, the diversity of input improves the overall team performance.

> ## The most important measure of how good a game I played was how much better I'd made my team-mates play.
>
> —Bill Russell, coach and Hall of Fame basketball player

❖ **Support**—Since teams are collaborative and goal oriented, the success of the team is critical to our individual success. For this reason, it is important to be supportive of other team members, give them credit for their actions, compliment them on successes, and help them in their difficulties. Remember how wild geese honked encouragement while in formation and helped each other in times of crisis? We should be just as supportive of our teams. Being supportive does not imply that we should not confront conflict within the team. It does imply that it should be done in a professional manner. Of course, being supportive requires our sharing the ownership of team actions whether positive or negative.

A Trust Issue

During the late 1990s, my organization outsourced much of its technology service delivery to a combination of four publicly owned organizations. Each of the organizations was prominent and highly successful as a separate entity. The services provided included desktop support, project development, service delivery support, and a national help desk. While a lead organization had been identified and the individual contracts had been drafted to clearly delineate the lines of responsibility, there were serious issues from the very beginning. To be effective, the four separate organizations needed to develop a team concept and deliver seamless service. Teamwork also requires trust and, often, a willingness to sacrifice personal goals for team's, success. Although the delineation of services was sound, the practical application was unworkable. Each service provider continuously sought work that crossed boundaries with other team members. Additionally, whenever there were problems, the initial response was to fix responsibility rather than work together to resolve the issue. This desire to fix responsibility resulted in constant finger-pointing, which eventually resulted in a lack of trust within the team. Needless to say, the team was ineffective, and the organization suffered simply because of this lack of trust. They were unwilling to practice simple team concepts.

Lesson: Importance of Trust

Although the competence of individual team members is critical, trust is essential. Build your character so that other team members will trust you and be comfortable that you will always act with integrity.

Specific circumstances or team requirements may dictate that some of these personal qualities be used more frequently than others. Similarly, additional qualities may be needed to perform certain tasks on specialized teams or under specific circumstances. However, the ten personal qualities are uniformly applicable and critical for success on teams within any organization.

Alone we can do so little; together we can do so much.

—Helen Keller (1880–1968), US writer and lecturer

Teamwork is seen frequently in insects, birds, and animals and is practiced extensively by migrating geese. Similarly, organizations utilize teams at some level to ensure that missions are accomplished. Since teams are so common and are required for success in all environments, we must ensure that we develop the skills necessary to be effective in our environment. Minimizing these skills is a sure recipe for failure in accomplishing personal, team, and organizational goals.

Snowflakes are one of nature's most fragile things, but just look what they can do when they stick together.

—Vesta M. Kelley

Chapter Nine

Environmental Awareness and White-Tailed Deer

The environment is everything that isn't me.

—Albert Einstein (1879–1955),
German-born US theoretical physicist

PRINCIPLE NINE
Maintain Knowledge of Organizational Environmental Issues and Ensure Compatibility with Personal Values.

Awareness of the White-Tailed Deer

The white-tailed deer, the number one big game animal in the United States, spends considerable time maintaining awareness of its surroundings. Since they are not true migrating animals, they traditionally live inside a one-square-mile area and maintain a knowledge of most topographical features in their home area. Because they are color blind, they focus on the slightest movement. In most cases, they see, hear, or smell predators long before they are seen. We see white-tailed deer in the wild almost exclusively with their heads up, surveying their surroundings. Their environmental awareness and keen perception are essential for their survival.

Lesson Inspired by Nature
The same environmental awareness and keen perception practiced by the white-tailed deer is necessary in your environment for you to succeed.

Know Your Environment

Awareness is essential to move freely, avoid hazards, and maintain compliance with environmental norms. In this context, awareness is maintaining knowledge, realizing factors, and understanding factions affecting the organizational environment in which we operate. It involves assessing the implication of these factors, understanding the organization's reaction, and positioning ourselves to respond in a positive and professional manner. We must always be aware of the organizational culture to ensure that our personal actions are consistent with expected norms. It is through knowing the factors, understanding the causes, assessing the implications, and adjusting our actions accordingly that we prepare to meet the organizational challenges.

Career Choice Implications

The latter years of my career were spent with the federal government. I was recruited, along with a small number of other external executive managers, to assist in reorganizing the agency into a more customer-focused organization. Congress granted the department the authority to recruit up to forty external executives for key positions to assist this effort. It was ironic that even during personal social events, some individuals would find a reason to politely excuse themselves from the conversation once they heard the name of my employer. It was obvious that there was something about the organization, a prior experience, or an employee contact that made them uncomfortable. I do not know whether it was the perceived intimate financial knowledge that the organization collected or the concern that any statement they made would eventually be used against them. Regardless, in some circles I was persona non grata. Even though I had neither involvement nor access to private personal information, this guilt by association was painfully obvious. My solace was in knowing that reform was the purpose of the appointment and my role was specific: to aid in developing a more customer-focused organization. Yes, the organization was misunderstood but not unethical. It was in this environment that I met and worked with some of the most ethical and dedicated employees encountered throughout my career.

> # Lesson: Perceptions of Others
> Understand the implications that your career choices may have on personal associations. Do not allow others' perceptions to negatively impact your performance, even though you may have some uncomfortable moments.

There are many factors and factions of which we should be aware in a professional organizational environment. Just as the white-tailed deer must be aware of all aspects of their surroundings for survival, we must be just as aware of every aspect of our environment to achieve success. We should know the impact the many factors and factions have on us, our goals, and eventually our careers. These factors and factions include (1) organizational goals, (2) organizational culture, (3) management, (4) peers, (5) project assignments, (6) office politics, and (7) other issues.

❖ **Organizational Goals**—We should be knowledgeable of the organization's mission, goals, and objectives. Since they are used to determine organizational direction, focus, and emphasis, they must be instrumental in shaping our actions. We should also be

- Aware of how the mission, goals, and objectives impact personnel, shareholders, customers, and the environment;

- Knowledgeable of what is important to the organization, and more importantly, understand how our roles assist in the accomplishment of its mission, goals, and objectives;

- Aware of the organization's ethical standards and how these standards affect the community in which it operates.

Our awareness of the organization, mission, goals, objectives, ethical standards, and environmental policies will enable us to maintain focus and gauge the compatibility of our goals with those of the organization.

❖ **Organizational Culture**—Every organization—public, private, service, or community—has a culture that is distinct. Organizational culture is the general thinking, action, focus, behavior, and approach to problem solving that distinguishes the organization from others. It is the general approach to problem solving, the treatment of its customers, and its relationship with the community. Organizational culture is also the internal and external communication, social mores, and relationship between management and employees. Culture is all inclusive, affects all aspects of the organization, becomes entrenched over time, and is maintained even as different employees enter and exit the organization.

Cultural Diversity

My assignment while living in a foreign country was working with groups from many other countries and cultures. One of my tasks was to change certain company financial reporting practices that had been developed over a number of years. This assignment provided my most visible lesson on the importance of being aware of your environment. Clearly the up-front, in-your-face management approach often practiced in our culture is a prescription for failure in many other cultures. My recognition of cultural differences to problem solving and my willingness to adjust my approach when working with people from those cultures was essential for success. I grouped the cultural diversity I encountered into six basic groups:

- **Suggestive**—In this group, explicit demands were seldom made. However, there were often severe consequences if the suggestions were not taken as directives.

- **Independent**—This group was very deliberate in their responsiveness. They searched for every angle to avoid compliance and often used national laws as the basis for their noncompliance. I was constantly justifying why national laws were not a factor to consider in complying with many of my requests.

- **Agreeable**—This group was most often agreeable and ideal for group consensus. They did not want to be perceived as disagreeable. However, it was much more difficult for me to get follow-through on promises. Continuous follow-up was required.

- **Supportive**—This group was quick to be supportive, but their actions were indirect. Others did not view them as major players. They often sought to be viewed as involved and on the cutting edge of every issue. However, their impact was minimized simply because of their lack of influence.

- **Confrontational**—This group allowed historical issues to make working together difficult. Being able to maintain civility and compliance were my only expectations.

- **Deliberate**—In this group, compliance was always assured but not always on a timely basis. I did not expect active involvement or an open dialogue from this group. They were unhurried and basically just followed along.

All of these groups were successful and effective in their environments; however, the differences were distinct. There were different approaches to problem solving, responsiveness, and team dynamics. I often thought of these cultural differences as an extension of the individual differences we see while working with people from the same cultural background. My effectiveness was dependent upon environmental awareness, the ability to recognize and accept the cultural differences, and the flexibility to adjust my actions accordingly

Lesson: Cultural Awareness

Awareness of your culture is critical, but strict adherence to your own cultural bias is not always the most effective approach. When working as part of a team, competency in other cultures, environmental awareness, and a flexible approach are essential for success.

Because of the many different organizational cultures, it is often difficult to merge two large professional organizations and expect these cultures to instantaneously operate in harmony. It is the cultural differences that create hurdles for many companies. After many years of understanding and operating in a known culture, employees are required to adapt to a different approach to even the most basic activities. These differences cause tremendous tension among people in the merged organizations. To be effective, the new organization must find common ground to increase the comfort level of employees before it can operate efficiently.

There are as many different cultures as there are organizations. When we observe organizations, some are very employee focused while others are production focused. Some organizations attempt to identify talent early and focus on developing that talent while others tend to promote employees based on years of experience. There are organizations that communicate effectively while others struggle with basic communication. Some are very open and informal while others are very sterile and extremely formal. Some organizations use the "up or out" approach (every professional employee is expected to advance toward leadership positions within a well-defined time frame or they are expected to leave) while others recognize the need for stable employees who perform well at all levels. Some are known for their unyielding integrity while others are more carefree and operate closer to the edge. This is not an exhaustive list of organizational cultures or an indication that any of these cultures are preferred or more successful. Instead, it is indicative of the many defining characteristics of organizations. Regardless of the culture, every organization must utilize its strengths to achieve success. Be sure that the organization's culture is compatible with your values and goals.

A Lasting Lesson

My first professional employment after completing my undergraduate degree was a management training position with a Fortune 100 company. The first month of training was designed to provide a broad overview of the organization. One of my first assignments was to shadow the region manager. During the weeklong experience, we had many fairly intense conversations that covered a wide range of topics and issues. Over the years, the substance of most of the conversations has faded from memory. However, one of his statements I have kept with me as a nugget. His comment was, "Bill, every company is a bastard, it is a matter of which bastard you choose to work with." While I would not necessarily describe organizations using his words, I do agree that every organization has its distinctiveness or its own culture. The choice we all must make is finding that culture in which we are comfortable. That is not to imply that the incompatible organizations are wrong. Instead, it is a matter of finding the fit with our ideals and beliefs.

Lesson on Compatibility

It is important that you work with an organization whose culture is compatible with your values. The potential for accomplishing your goals and achieving success will be significantly improved.

It is important to maintain an awareness of the organization's culture and how it manifests itself. Remember how the white-tailed deer practices this awareness? We must be just as effective at practicing awareness in our environment. Since we spend a significant amount of our time thinking about, planning, or performing organizational activities, finding an organization with a culture that enables us to grow, develop, and pursue our goals is essential for success. If we find compatibility with the organization's culture and our personal values, it positively affects our relationship with family and friends. It also improves our ongoing disposition. We must ask several questions if there is incompatibility:

- Can I adjust my personal values and be comfortable in the organization?

- If I make the adjustment, can I accomplish my goals in an uncomfortable environment?

It is very unlikely that an adjustment of personal values can be made effectively. Therefore, considering a more compatible organization is the most likely solution.

When selecting an organization to advance our career, be aware of those in which the public has a negative perception. There is a tendency for the public to project that negative perception on all employees because of the association. There is a presumption of guilt by association regardless of the personal integrity of individual employees.

Guilt by Association

The initial impression by many in the general public is that the entire senior team at Enron was dishonest, causing its downfall. The courts have proven and some members of the senior team have acknowledged that there was some wrongdoing. However, there were probably many individuals who were not involved, had no personal knowledge of the alleged wrongdoing, and who continued to maintain strong personal integrity throughout the ordeal. In spite of their personal integrity, they will always carry a label of guilt by association in spite of their innocence.

> ## Lesson on Ethical Assessments
>
> If you sense there are unethical standards in your organization, avoid involvement, determine the potential implications, and assess the personal impact. You should always seek employment in an organization with strong ethical values that are compatible with yours to avoid being branded as unethical.

Divorce is very prevalent in our society. It often results from a difference in philosophy, lack of compatibility, a poor understanding of the partner, or many other reasons. Because of these differences, a decision is made by the participants to separate and go in different directions; so it is with professional organizations. Sometimes, after gaining additional knowledge, we determine that there is a lack of compatibility between the organization's customs and our values. We then decide to go in different directions. Regardless of the circumstances, it is important to always leave the organization on a positive note and never burn bridges. There are many reasons to avoid conflict, but the most important are that it accomplishes nothing and that it could negatively affect future employment. In departing, accept that the company may not be misdirected or wrong. Instead, it may be that the organization's and our personal beliefs, goals or direction are incompatible.

Public Perception in the Mid-70s

Much of my career was spent with a Fortune 50 company in the petroleum industry. During the early- to mid-70s, oil prices began to increase dramatically and the public perception was that petroleum companies were being extremely dishonest. The public perception was that

- There was not an oil shortage;

- Prices were artificially inflated;

- Petroleum companies were gouging customers.

Even in social situations, I was constantly bombarded with questions and insinuations about the lack of ethics in the industry. In fact, because of the public's accusation of guilt by association, I often refused to reveal my employer or even acknowledge association with the industry. Obviously, I was interested in the truth. Was my employer and the industry unethical, or was the news media portraying the negative image to the public? Because of my financial background and involvement with the organization's financial records, I was able to conclude that it was not an integrity issue. During that period, my company was actually incurring a significantly higher cost for raw material in arm's-length transactions with third parties. While I cannot speak for the industry, the profit for my employer was not substantially changed during this period. The increased consumer prices were caused by increased raw material costs, government price controls, and taxes. While this did not address the industry issue, this knowledge provided me with a level of comfort. In spite of the news media's portrayal and the public's perception, I saw no evidence of ethical misconduct. Yes, the industry and my employer, as part of that industry, had done a horrible job of communicating to the general public, but poor communication alone does not imply a breach of ethical standards.

Lesson on Public Perception

Understand the rationale for the public perception of your organization. It could be a forewarning of a difficult period for the organization, an ethical issue, or a misguided public perception. The knowledge will enable you to make the personal decision necessary to continue pursuing your career goals.

❖ **Management**—It is necessary to be aware of what is on management's radar screen. Be knowledgeable of the issues that management has identified as high priorities and those that are critical for the success of the organization. This knowledge will enable us to position ourselves and focus our effort in areas where we can get the greatest return.

We must also learn and appreciate the language of management. This knowledge is necessary to improve our communication. Moreover, it is essential to be effective in our responsiveness. Every profession has a language that is unique, although practical, when used with peers in the profession. However, it is extremely difficult to communicate to a wider audience using professional or technical jargon. Yes, it is important to understand the technical issues and be able to converse with others within the profession. However, this jargon must be translated into the language of management to communicate effectively with the wider audience. Success is often dependent upon the effectiveness in which we master this skill.

The Glazed Look

Some years ago, my organization was acquired by a foreign company. There were technical accounting differences caused by specific countries' requirements that made the financial results different between the two organizations. I was asked to explain these differences to the board of directors of my organization. Naturally, I was elated at the opportunity and spent considerable time preparing what I thought was a powerful presentation. It will forever remain etched in my mind the glazed look that slowly emerged on the board members' faces as I discussed the differences. I failed miserably because I was attempting to explain the differences using terminology that was unique to the accounting profession. I failed to translate the technical jargon into a language that my audience could understand. Fortunately, the chairman unknowingly rescued me by stating they were short on time and would continue the discussion of the topic at a later meeting.

> ## Lesson: Awareness of Management Needs
> Effectiveness is determined by not only your professional knowledge but by your ability to translate that knowledge into a more universal language: the language of management.

It is essential to be aware of who the decision makers are in the organization. Every organization has hierarchical charts that are recognized as the official chain of command. However, it is just as important to recognize that not all major decisions are made in a manner consistent with that outlined in the formal organizational chart. Many decisions are delegated or assumed by others outside of the formal process. Recognizing this informal structure and adjusting responsiveness accordingly is necessary to avoid running afoul in the organization.

A Complex Process

There were times in my organization when the hierarchical organizational charts bore little resemblance to the way the organization operated. Yes, there were international implications, but it was difficult at times to understand the process. For example, there were the following complexities:

- An international parent-company structure directing total operations.

- An international business structure directing each of the major business organizations.

- A national structure with indirect responsibility for operations in the country.

- A national business structure with responsibility for the country's business operations.

- International organizations for nonbusiness operations with indirect authority (i.e., human resources).

- A national organization for nonbusiness operations responsibility for the country's activities.

In fact, the ongoing joke in the organization was, if someone gives directions, salute first, then find out his or her role. There were some initial adjustments required. Many employees found the adjustment difficult and chose to leave the organization. In spite of the complexity and the lack of a clearly defined hierarchical organizational chart, the organization operated effectively because employees adapted to the new structure.

> ## Lesson: Understanding Structure
> **It is important to understand the decision-making process in your organization. Success or failure is dependent upon your ability to adjust and work within both the formal and informal structures.**

With this awareness of management's agenda, the decision makers, the major organizational concerns, and the prime areas of focus, we can better direct our efforts and effectively discharge our responsibilities.

❖ **Peers**—Our peers are our competitors. However, we must recognize and accept them as our teammates. We see this same competitive yet collaborative dynamic in the lifestyle of white-tailed deer, and they appear to survive quite comfortably. We should be just as effective. While it is generally accepted that competition brings out the best in us and that teamwork is essential for success, it is just as important to avoid fraternizing with the enemy. Drawing the balance between the competitor and teammate dilemma is the art that must be mastered to maintain effectiveness within an organization.

Since our peers are often competing for the same advancement or positions, it is important to be aware of this competitiveness. This is not suggesting that competition is a reason for jealousy, envy, or infighting. Instead, it is a natural result of organizational structures that must be considered. Awareness of the progress of our peers can also be used as a means of determining our organizational progress. While their advancement should not be the sole factor in gauging our success, it can be used as a barometer to ensure that our advancement is, at a minimum, on par with others. This is not suggesting that we develop adversarial relationships or that we use them to our advantage. Instead, we must maintain professionalism and treat our peers with the utmost respect while maintaining awareness of their organizational progress.

From a teammate perspective, it is critical that we develop a relationship and work with our peers for the accomplishment of organizational goals. We must be cooperative, supportive, and professional at all times. We gain knowledge of organizational norms, customs, and practices from them and utilize the knowledge to advance our careers. Additionally, because of the organization's team concept, it is almost impossible to succeed without developing a professional working relationship with our peers.

❖ **Project Assignments**—Maintaining an awareness of critical or high-profile projects and the pattern of assignment is also necessary. Since these projects provide the opportunity for exposure, knowing and understanding the rationale for how these assignments are made is critical. We must stay involved in the high-profile projects to maintain visibility with key decision makers. There is no substitute for face time. Without involvement, performance, and visibility, it is extremely difficult to demonstrate the commitment, skill, and dedication necessary for continued organizational advancement. Inquire about and clearly understand the rationale for decisions, especially if we see a pattern where we are constantly assigned low-visibility projects. While project assignment should not be considered the sole criterion to measure the organization's perceptions of our performance, it can be used as one of the barometers.

❖ **Office Politics**—In this context, office politics is the activity used by individuals or groups to communicate, gather information, inform, win over, or gain an advantage over another. Yes, office politics can be either productive or, often, counterproductive. It is misleading to categorize all office politics as counterproductive since there is a significant amount of positive information shared daily. However, oftentimes the information gathering or communication is used deviously, disparagingly, or for personal benefit. Always avoid discussions related to other personnel, personal information, and confidential organizational matters. These discussions are often designed to gather information, which eventually leads to gossiping or petty politics. Since discussion on the topics does not promote personal growth, contribute to the effectiveness of the team, or advance the organization's goals, it is important to avoid involvement. That being said, there is some politics in everything we do in life, and the organization is no exception.

The entire awareness issue could fall into the category of politics since we spend a considerable amount of time gathering information and using that information for personal gain. In spite of this, it is always important to know the following:

- The organization's goals and objectives

- The major players

- The alignment of the major players

- Where the power is wielded

- The expectations of the team members

Gathering this information could be classified as office politics since it is gained primarily through open discussion with peers. It is also used for personal gain. However, this is productive office politics. It is only through an intimate knowledge of this organizational information that we navigate efficiently and ensure becoming an effective member of the team. The challenge we have is to distinguish between petty politics and information gathering. The key is to ensure that our involvement is for positive purposes.

❖ **Other Issues**—Other organizational issues that we should also be aware of include the following:

- We must be aware that regardless of our diplomacy, integrity, and professionalism, conflict will often emerge because of misinformation, greed, envy, or jealousy. In spite of the concerted effort to avoid conflict, there will be individual differences because of the competitive environment. Therefore, we must continuously build bridges to minimize the impact.

- There are many outspoken and silent supporters in the organization that we can depend on based on the level of commitment, integrity, perseverance, and professionalism we display. Be aware, acknowledge these supporters, and build on other relationships such that support is always available when needed.

- We must be aware of the perceptions that others, especially decision makers, have of us, our performance, our work ethic, and our professionalism. Since they determine our organizational progress, we must always ensure we leave a positive impression.

- We must be aware of and continuously search for critical, yet unwritten, information that is essential for continued growth. All essential and significant information, such as organizational norms, customs, and practices, is not always neatly catalogued and available for review.

Every organization is distinct, with customs, practices, and other areas of differences. White-tailed deer spend an enormous amount of time maintaining awareness of their environment. For them, environmental awareness is critical for survival and is a life-or-death issue. We should be just as diligent in observing our environment, monitoring the organization's activities, reviewing management's decisions, and aligning our actions to ensure we maintain our effectiveness. Although maintaining awareness of the organizational environment and reacting appropriately is not a life-or-death issue for us, it is essential for our success.

Do not look back in anger or forward in fear, but around in awareness.

—James Thurber (1894–1961), US humorist and illustrator

Chapter Ten

Aggressive Patience and Crocodiles

Things may come to those who wait, but only the things left by those who hustle.

—Abraham Lincoln (1809–1865), US president and politician

Patience is not passive: on the contrary it is active; it is concentrated strength.

—Author unknown

PRINCIPLE TEN
Advocate When Necessary and Pause When Required.

The Aggressive Patience of the Crocodile

Although crocodiles are known for their aggressiveness in pursuing their prey, surprising and explosive attacks, powerful lunges, and invincible strikes, these actions are a small fraction of their lives. In the wild, they may consume no more than one hundred meals a year. They bask in the sun to soak up warmth to power their metabolism. However, the cornerstone of their success is patience or inactivity for long periods. They lie motionless for most of the day, and this inactivity enables them to conserve and redirect their energy toward keeping themselves alive. Their aggressiveness in defending their territory, capturing prey, and patience in using energy for other useful purposes distinguishes the crocodile from many other reptiles.

Lesson Inspired by Nature

You must learn a lesson from the crocodile. Be extremely aggressive when necessary to advance your career. However, be patient at other times on less important issues. More importantly, know when to be aggressive and when to be patient.

Let us be up and doing, with a heart for any fate; still achieving, still pursuing, learn to labor and to wait.

—Henry Wadsworth Longfellow (1807–1882),
US poet and writer

148

Controlled Aggression and Assertive Patience

The very name "aggressive patience" seems to be an oxymoron and may seem perplexing, as it is difficult to understand how we can be both aggressive and patient simultaneously. Aggressive patience, in this context, is the need to maintain a level of aggressiveness on some very specific issues but to practice patience on other issues. It is advocating vociferously for the advancement of our careers while practicing patience on some of the more mundane issues that are less career threatening. I hesitate to include patience as a success factor primarily because it is often used in a stereotypical manner to degrade some ethnic groups. However, I would advocate that we cannot exclude either aggressiveness or patience as critical success factors. There will be ample opportunities to practice both at different junctures in our career. In fact, success dictates that we utilize both at different intervals and, more importantly, assures that they are utilized appropriately.

Aggressive patience means that we must be aggressive in being advocates for ourselves and those things necessary to ensure the success of our career. However, it also means that we must be patient and recognize that success may not occur as quickly as we would like. Be aggressive in keeping ourselves in the forefront for opportunities yet patient enough to avoid becoming an annoyance in the pursuit of these opportunities. We must be aggressive in seeking opportunities and patient enough to recognize that every opportunity sought will not be forthcoming. We must be aggressive in ensuring we have the necessary skills and patient enough to know that skills alone will not be the only deciding factor. Be aggressive in ensuring that we are forces to be acknowledged but patient enough to avoid becoming forces to be removed. Be aggressive enough to keep ourselves abreast of external market opportunities yet patient enough to recognize that not every opportunity is as lucrative as it appears. We must be aggressive enough to be extremely disappointed when we fail to advance but patient enough to recognize that we will not receive every available opportunity. Be aggressive in establishing stretch goals and patient in maintaining focus, and recognize that success requires extraordinary performance. The key to our success is to follow the example of the crocodile and know when to be aggressive and when to be patient.

It takes time to excel because success is merely the natural reward of taking time to do anything well.

—Joseph Ross, US motivational writer

Inappropriate Aggression

A colleague tells the story of a new hire he brought into his organization at a level that enabled him to compete for an upcoming manager selection. Obviously, the decision was not received well by the existing potential candidates. However, they were respectful of the decision and professional with the new hire. Mitch, one of the potential manager candidates, later discovered that the salary of the new hire was higher than his. Perceived salary inequities are by far the greatest source of unhappiness in most organizations, and this was no exception. As expected, Mitch was upset and wrote a letter to his manager demanding an explanation, requesting a salary increase, and threatening to quit if the increase was not granted. He also shared the memo with purported friends and became very vocal in criticizing the situation and his manager. Mitch's public actions were designed to cause considerable embarrassment to the manager. Unfortunately, his actions were very immature. There was absolutely nothing wrong with Mitch's decision to address a personal concern with his manager. His error was in trying to resolve it publicly. Because of the embarrassment and limited alternatives available, the manager accepted Mitch's threat to leave the organization.

Lesson: Manage Your Aggression

It is quite appropriate to be aggressive in addressing troublesome issues. However, you must remain professional at all times. Public resolution of a personal issue is never an acceptable practice. Instead, these issues must be resolved privately. Uncontrolled aggression is a quick way to limit your career.

Aggressive patience does not imply that we should sit back, remain idle, and wait for opportunities to suddenly appear. This listless approach is a sure recipe for failure. It leaves the impression that we are either satisfied with our current status, not sincere, uninterested, or lack ambition. A major reason often given for overlooking individuals for advancement is the lack of motivation or drive. We must be proactive at all times in marketing and promoting ourselves, our commitment, our ability, and our willingness to accept more challenging opportunities.

Even if you are on the right track, you'll get run over if you just sit there.

—Will Rogers (1879–1935), US mayor, entertainer, and journalist

In spite of our best efforts, there will be occasions when we are not selected for a much sought-after position. Often, the first reaction after being overlooked for a logical promotion is to adopt the aggressive, rather than the passive, behaviors exhibited by the crocodile. Our initial reaction is to immediately pursue opportunities outside of the current organization. While that may be the best decision, there are a number of questions we should ask ourselves before taking that drastic step:

- Were my expectations too high?

- Was the selected candidate more qualified?

- Will there be other opportunities available soon?

- Where do I rank in relation to my peers?

- What was the major reason I was not selected?

- Was the opportunity consistent with my goals?

- Is there additional personal preparation that I should consider?

- Was there an inherent message in the selection?

By asking these questions, we may be able to understand the rationale for the decision and avoid making a rash, career-altering decision. Additionally, we should consider consulting with a trusted advisor for external input or guidance on our next steps. Transferring organizations may provide tremendous advantages. However, before departing, we should exercise patience, review the implications, assess potential future internal opportunities, and understand the entire promotional process. The important factor is to avoid an overreaction.

Patience: It's Essential

Over the years, my organization grew substantially, creating many employee growth opportunities. I served as a mentor for Jerry, an individual recruited directly out of undergraduate school. He was young, aggressive, talented, and interested in pursuing a management career in the financial organization. His interest in preparation was evident in the pursuit and receipt of his Certified Public Accountant (CPA) certification shortly after joining the organization. Six months later, a manager position became available in my largest area, and Jerry asked to be considered for the position. I explained that he needed more experience leading projects before moving into this demanding and highly visible position. Unfortunately, Jerry disagreed, expressed his disagreement in a personally derogatory manner, and quit his position on the spot. Although I was impressed with his aggressiveness in identifying, preparing for, and pursuing his goals, and understood his interest in advancement, I had some major issues with his actions:

- His decision to quit was irrational and not based on objective thought.

- He had an inflated impression of himself and his preparation.

- He was unable to listen to reason.

- He lacked patience in pursuing his goals.

- He did not demonstrate the ability to manage himself.

- He chose to burn bridges rather than take the high road or a rational approach.

Had Jerry practiced more patience, I believe he could have had a successful career with the organization. Several years later, I received a letter, followed by a telephone call from him, acknowledging his irrational decision and apologizing for his behavior. In spite of that, over the years, I received three separate requests for employment verification because Jerry was changing organizations. I often wondered if those job changes resulted from irrational decisions. My hope is that he eventually realized his potential and achieved his goal.

Lesson: Be Realistic

It is important to always be aggressive in identifying, preparing for, and pursuing your goals. However, it is essential to maintain a realistic view of your readiness for promotional opportunities. You must be aggressive when necessary and exercise patience when required to enhance your career opportunities.

Do not use a hatchet to remove a fly from your friend's forehead.

—Chinese proverb

Aggression is often perceived as a measure of confidence or assuredness. Likewise, aggression can often be negatively perceived as forward, pushy, or even tactless. In spite of the potential for misperceptions, it is still quite necessary to continuously be aggressive in the pursuit of goals. The key, however, is to ensure the aggression is measured, controlled, and focused.

Hasten slowly.

—Augustus Caesar (63 BC–AD 14), Roman emperor

Patience is also required as we pursue advancement opportunities. After a significant investment in preparation, it is understandable that we expect significant opportunities to be readily available. However, we must also recognize that many of our contemporaries have made similar investments and expect the same advancement opportunities. Patience is recognizing that our accomplishments, although significant, are not uniquely different from others. There will be other individuals with similar or greater skills and experiences. Let me quickly add that this is not to suggest that we reduce our expectations, lose confidence, or accept a secondary status. I am suggesting that we maintain awareness of circumstances, evaluate the implications, and adjust our plans accordingly.

Patience and fortitude conquer all things.

—Ralph Waldo Emerson (1803–1882), US essayist, poet, and philosopher

Although we should be patient and not expect to begin our careers at the top of the organization, we must be confident that with diligence and hard work the road to the top is unimpaired. Also, be aware that there are many other factors affecting organizational advancement such as demonstrating a strong work ethic, exhibiting loyalty, displaying commitment, and showing allegiance to the organization's goals and objectives. Yes, it is understandable that most organizations require some observation of readiness. Yet, it is just as understandable that our objective should be to seek every opportunity for organizational advancement. Because of this dichotomy, continuously seek opportunities and recognize that demonstrated skills, experience, aggressiveness, and patience are also essential for advancement.

Patience Rewarded

At the time of my return from a foreign assignment, the organization was in the midst of a reorganization and related reduction in workforce. As a result, there was not a position readily available that matched my background and experience. My initial reaction was dismay, followed closely by anger. The result was an aggressively worded letter asking the organization to fulfill its promise of a comparable position after a foreign assignment. If such a position was not available, I asked senior officials to provide me with a financial package and release me from the organization. Clearly, the release was not ideal. At the same time, I was not sure how I would continue to pursue my goals in a holding position. During several subsequent face-to-face meetings, the senior executive refused my request for a financial package and suggested that he was confident a meaningful opportunity would be available. I had a dilemma—should I wait based on his statement, which was not an assurance, or pursue opportunities elsewhere? Remember the patient crocodile? My decision was to exercise patience and also to begin preparing to pursue other opportunities. Fortunately, a position became available within three months that was a substantial promotion and clearly in line with my goals. In this case, I was extremely aggressive in pursuing my goals and demonstrating the eagerness and willingness to assume greater responsibility. I was also patient in not overreacting to what later proved to be a temporary misalignment of personnel.

Lesson on Aggressive Patience

Be aggressive in the pursuit of your goals, but understand that the organization may not act in accordance with your plan. Patience is sometimes necessary to achieve success.

There are many opportunities where aggression is essential to promote the advancement of personal goals. Similarly, there are numerous circumstances where patience is clearly the preferred option. In their natural habitat, crocodiles have perfected the practice of knowing when to be aggressive and when to be patient. It is essential for their survival. The key to our success is just as dependent upon knowing when to unleash our aggressiveness and when to maintain patience.

He that can have patience can have what he will.

—Benjamin Franklin (1706–1790), US statesman and writer

Chapter Eleven

Communication
and Whales

Every message you send provides information about
you as a worker, a team player, a potential leader, or
a potential problem.

—Eric Maisel, PhD,
US psychotherapist, writer, and author

PRINCIPLE ELEVEN
Develop and Maintain Effective Verbal, Nonverbal, Listening, and Interaction Skills.

Effective Communication of Whales

Even though we do not often think of whales as great communicators, their skills are distinct, recognizable, and varied:

- **Singing**—Their vocal repertoire is complex, and their range covers as many as seven octaves.

- **Respect**—They are extremely polite in their conversations and rarely interrupt one another.

- **Touch**—Their social touching is a significant communication tool.

- **Sounds**—They have distinct dialects, and their sounds can be detected for many miles.

- **Emotions**—They use hard slaps of the tail, flippers, or head when disturbed or angry.

- **Listening Skills**—They are extremely quiet when predators are near.

Even though the ability to create and detect sounds is the primary communication system, they also display other interaction skills that render their system effective.

Words are, of course the most powerful drug used by mankind.

—Rudyard Kipling (1865–1936), British poet and writer

Develop Effective Skills

Effective communication is the great equalizer that can bridge gaps, or it can be the unfortunate schism that leads to the demise of otherwise capable individuals. Often, the focus of communication is centered on the effectiveness of verbal skills. In addition to verbal skills, developing strong listening skills and mastering nonverbal actions are essential for effective communication. It is impossible to be an effective communicator without mastering all three essential skills.

Verbal communication is the primary manner that humans use to express themselves, articulate thoughts, and relay ideas to others. The focus on verbal communication begins very early in life and is the primary basis on which a child's development is measured. It is expected that a child will learn to speak, begin developing multisyllabic words, and begin developing sentences at certain stages of development. However, since children are not born with communication skills, we must speculate on their thoughts and disposition. So it is with individuals who have excellent verbal skills but who fail to articulate their thoughts. These nonverbal individuals are misunderstood, lose the opportunity to make valuable contributions, and fail to promote their personal goals.

Communication is one of the most important skills needed for success in any organization since it is often used as the basis for measuring other skills. It is possible and quite commonplace to see individuals with many outstanding qualities who fail to distinguish themselves because of inadequate communication skills. Similarly, a command of these skills often distinguishes some individuals and pushes them ahead of other talented individuals. The perception of ability is often identified more with communication skills than with other phases of job performance. Mastering the art of communication must be achieved to advance in most organizations.

Communication is, unquestionably, an important ingredient for individual success. It is also one of the single biggest causes of failure. Many individuals get so involved with the tremendous responsibilities of daily activities that they fail to recognize the importance of continuous, effective communication. The result is that valuable information is unavailable, organizational performance is impaired, and the individual's performance is adversely affected. Avoiding communication is damaging to the individual, the team, and the organization.

Whatever your goal or position, if you know how and when to speak, and when to remain silent, your chances of success are proportionately increased.

—Ralph C. Smedley (1878–1965), founder, Toastmasters International

Mastering communication skills in most organizations must be directionally focused. The focus must be in a minimum of three separate directions, each requiring different content, emphasis, and frequency: (1) upward, (2) across, and (3) downward.

❖ **Upward**—Upward communication is the ongoing dialogue we have with the decision makers in the organization or the group of individuals who are above us in the management structure. Since these decision makers evaluate our job performance and determine our rate of advancement, it is essential that they see us as effective, communicators. Upward communication is more about information sharing and is focused on project planning, summarizing results, reviewing status, and other performance-related issues. To be effective, we must use phrases that are clear, focused, concise, succinct, and professionally delivered. It does not matter what level we are in the organization or the significance of the assignment, it is our responsibility to tailor our communications to the audience. We must understand management's expectations, vision, goals, thoughts, and emphasis and adjust our communications to be responsive to these objectives. Upward communication should never be approached cavalierly. Instead, it should be directed toward demonstrating confidence and leaving a positive impression on the audience.

Upward Communication

Since organizations are unique in their style, it is important to determine the most effective method of communicating in your organization. A practice I followed for many years was to develop a set of monthly, quarterly, and annual performance objectives that outlined projects, major focus areas, and expected completion dates. This information was provided to management to get buy-in and to ensure there was a clear understanding of where my work would be focused. At least monthly, I reported the status of each objective upward in a management report that also highlighted other accomplishments and pending issues. I always arranged a follow-up verbal discussion to ensure the written points were registered and to allow the opportunity for questions. It was a way of ensuring buy-in from management and showing them that my focus was on the appropriate issues. It was also a means of ensuring that the status of projects was well known and that the lines of upward communication remained open.

Lesson on Upward Communication

Determine the most effective method of communicating upward in your organization and follow that practice consistently. It is essential that you keep the lines of communication open at all times.

❖ **Across**—Communication entails relationship building, team building, and information sharing. Communication across is directed toward our coworkers or the individuals maintaining similar positions and responsibilities in the organization. Although our peers may not be a part of the decision-makers' chain, effective communication and interaction with this group is significant and can greatly impact our progression. Since organizations are dependent upon teams and teamwork requires effective communication, it is impossible to operate effectively in an organization without open and honest communication with peers. Maintaining isolation or attempting to avoid communicating with the group is extremely shortsighted and definitely a recipe for failure. Additionally, we must continue to cultivate these relationships since they are often needed for support, information, and assistance. Decision makers often use the interaction we demonstrate with this group as a measure of our ability to coexist and build effective teams and relationships. Because of its organizational significance, effective communication across the organization is essential.

Peer Communication

I was often involved with teams that provided internal support services to the organization. Because of this, we had significantly less direct contact with external customers. It was imperative that we maintained an extremely close and strong communication link with all levels in the organization. Our objective was to make sure they were always aware of issues, projects, concerns, and the level of support my team was providing. To enhance this communication, I prepared a brief one-page document outlining key projects and the current status along with other pertinent information. This document was distributed and discussed weekly with my peers at staff meetings to ensure information was current and available for dissemination throughout the organization. The underlying purpose was to ensure that the information flow was open, current, accurate, timely, and flowing freely throughout the organization. This simple information-management strategy was designed to ensure that I controlled the information. More importantly, the information was factual and frequent, which removed uncertainty and created a positive image in the organization.

Lesson on Assertive Communication

Be assertive and ensure that information about you and your programs is factual, precise, timely, and widely distributed. Open communication is powerful and can be one important means of controlling your destiny.

❖ **Downward**—Communication to this group entails information sharing, task assignment, and performance feedback. This is the group of employees that we supervise, manage, or have the responsibility for ensuring their development in the organization. This is the group that perceives us as being the organization and looks to us for information, guidance, and direction. Because of their dependence on us, it is imperative that we maintain effective communication and establish ourselves as responsive, trustworthy, reliable, and fair. In their eyes, our actions define the organization's integrity. In numerous personnel surveys, it has been determined that employees trust their immediate manager much more than any other level of management. Because of this, it is important that we, as leaders, maintain and foster the trust that employees place in us. It is important that they are kept informed and that the lines of communication remain open, even if the news is negative. It is also important to praise generously, criticize both artfully and privately, and communicate frequently, factually, and with integrity.

Communicating with Employees

For many years, I had management responsibility that included direct employee supervision. In the early years, I had few employees to supervise, which enabled communication to be maintained on a one-on-one basis. Most mornings, regardless of the job time pressures, I would visit and speak with each employee personally before beginning my day. As time passed, the employees expected the early exchanges. On those days that I did not visit, some would stop by my office to engage in that brief dialogue. The purpose of my morning visitations was to dialogue with each employee on his or her own turf, remove barriers, and open the lines of communication. It also enabled me to listen to employees, understand their issues and concerns, and provide brief feedback on project difficulties. It provided them with an opportunity to identify issues or offer suggestions. More importantly, it created a sense of value for them as team members.

As the years passed, my responsibilities increased, and the number of employees I managed increased. The daily one-on-one dialogue could no longer be maintained. Although the number of employees I managed increased and the number of locations expanded dramatically, I continued to believe in the importance of open dialogue. For this reason, I continued to maintain open lines of communication through frequent field trips to conduct both small and large group discussions. The purpose was to always maintain a dialogue with employees on their turf or as close to it as possible. By listening, I understood their issues and could address them as they developed rather than waiting until they mushroomed into monumental problems.

Lesson: Building Relationships through Communication

It is important to communicate with others openly, frequently, frankly, and in a comfortable environment. When you reach out, you improve the dialogue and project a caring image.

Communicating with a Large, Dispersed Group

In government, my employee base was extremely large and widely dispersed in many offices throughout the United States. As a result, effective communication, including open dialogue, became much more of a challenge. Communication was just as important in these larger groups. Unfortunately, it was impossible to maintain the one-on-one dialogue because of the geographic dispersion. Yet, the objectives remained the same:

- Communicate with employees.

- Ensure there is a vehicle for upward communication.

- Ensure communication across lines of responsibility.

- Maintain a working team relationship.

- Ensure employees are informed of developments within the organization.

To ensure successful communication, I adopted the following practices:

- Personal visits to employee locations became a major focus of my time and effort. There was a series of town hall meetings with employees at each location visited. The majority of the meetings were spent responding to questions, listening to concerns, and providing the opportunity for dialogue. As time passed, the openness of these meetings increased tremendously. They were important for me since they enabled me to keep a pulse on the mood of employees, provided a better understanding of the organization's issues, and ensured a vehicle for disseminating information. The meetings were also invaluable because they gave employees the opportunity to have input, express themselves, and, more importantly, feel more like a part of the organization.

- An "Ask Bill" electronic forum was developed that allowed employees to inquire about issues and concerns or just offer comments directly. While this forum could never replace one-on-one dialogue, it provided employees the opportunity to communicate upward. I read and personally responded to many questions and ensured that every other inquiry received a prompt response. The "Ask Bill" forum was used heavily, especially by those offices where frequent visits were impossible. Although there were nuisance comments, there were also gems that came through this communication system.

- Each month, a letter was developed on a central topic or a series of topics and distributed electronically to each employee in the organization. The purpose was to ensure that pertinent information was conveyed directly rather than by hearsay. This communication method provided a greater likelihood that the right story was portrayed. It also kept employees informed of current organizational developments. These letters were supplemented with quarterly newsletters and periodic video-conferences followed by question-and answer-sessions.

Needless to say, employee communication is essential for us and must be a major focus regardless of our other organizational priorities. It is critical that these lines of communication remain open since it is the employees who have primary responsibility for discharging the organization's roles and responsibilities.

Lesson on Communication Strategy

You must develop a thorough communication strategy that will be effective in your organization. Employees are the performers. Since we rely on them, we must communicate effectively to ensure that high morale and strong performance are maintained.

While communication in every direction is important and the objective of connecting with the audience is the same, the approach is entirely different. Even within the groups, there is no one method that will be effective in every organization, every group, or for every occasion. Therefore, it is important to understand the channels of communication and develop a strategy that will enhance communication in each.

There are other habits that are just as important as verbal skills and must be developed before we can be classified as competent communicators. We must be just as effective as whales in practicing these communication, habits. Some of these habits are (1) listening, (2) conciseness, (3) nonverbal communication, (4) open-mindedness, and (5) respect.

❖ **Listening**—In an organizational environment, an effective communicator must be a good listener in addition to maintaining verbalization skills. You will recall that whales demonstrate tremendous listening skills. We must also develop our listening skills, be able to hear what is in the hearts and minds of others, and be willing to address these relevant issues. Effective listening encompasses the following:

- It involves listening to others without being judgmental.

- It entails hearing and understanding what is relevant to others.

- It includes empathizing with the thoughts and showing compassion for the ideas of others.

- It requires allowing others to complete their comments uninterrupted.

- It embodies respecting the comments of others, even though we may disagree.

Even though many different points of view may be presented, effective communication requires the ability to listen without showing contempt. Without the listening skill, individuals are often categorized as insensitive or uncaring. As a result, they fail to connect with their audience, thereby rendering themselves ineffective. Additionally, the organization and the team suffer because of a lack of involvement, and the individual suffers as an ineffective communicator.

Nature has given us two ears, two eyes, and but one tongue to the end we should hear and see more than we speak.

—Socrates (469–399 BC), Greek philosopher and educational performer

❖ **Conciseness**—Maintaining clarity while being concise and direct is also a requirement for effective communication. In organizations, most people would prefer communications be short and on point. The expectation is that the presenter will decipher and remove unimportant facts or other extraneous information. It is important to summarize information to avoid presenting all the laborious details and losing the audience. The speaker must be concise, or the audience fails to receive the critical points being conveyed, which results in a loss of effectiveness. Being concise takes more time to develop, but it has far more effect on the targeted audience. The point is, to become an effective communicator, take the time to ensure that both written and oral communications are both concise and focused at all times.

> **If you want to give a superb presentation, you need a powerful start and a dynamic ending, and you need to put them as close together as possible.**
>
> —Winston Churchill (1874–1965),
> British prime minister, statesman, and writer

❖ **Nonverbal Communication**—Nonverbal communication is the display of actions that communicate thoughts or feelings without verbalizing. Remember how whales use nonverbal actions to express their emotions? It is the actions that we display, either knowingly or unknowingly, that enable others to gauge the sincerity, commitment, or patience with the information being communicated or received. Facial expressions, body positions, and attentiveness all communicate just as directly as our words. These nonverbal cues are continuously being observed by our communication partners. With the most effective communicators, verbal communication is enhanced and supported by their nonverbal cues. If the verbal and nonverbal aspects fail to dovetail, the intended audience is left frustrated and confused. Since the audience can clearly observe the conflict, it undermines the effectiveness of the communicator.

The most important thing in communications is to hear what isn't being said.

—Peter Drucker, writer, management consultant, and professor

❖ **Open-Mindedness**—Open-mindedness is the willingness to be attentive to others' thoughts and opinions and to acknowledge that their input also has merit. It is the capability to hear others' thoughts and be amenable to accept and consider the input before drawing a final conclusion. It is self-aggrandizing to believe that we have all of the original thoughts or ideas. When the communicator is truly open minded and projects the openness to others, it allows for a more robust dialogue and a more informed decision. Effective communication requires an open exchange of thoughts and ideas rather than a one-way dialogue. A sure way to stifle communication is to enter the dialogue with a closed mind and project that image to other participants. It leaves the impression with the target audience of being communicated *to*, not communicated *with*.

❖ **Respect**—Every individual, regardless of their position, deserves respect from others. Remember how whales are extremely polite in their communication and rarely interrupt another? We must be just as respectful in our dealings. A genuine respect for others and their comments is required to develop effective communication. It is not important that the participants always agree. It is important to be courteous and avoid stifling the lines of communication. Since our thoughts, opinions, and ideas are shaped by our environment, our experiences, and our education, they will be distinctively different. If the communicator projects an image of lack of respect, it negatively impacts the willingness to share and reduces the likelihood of a free exchange of ideas. If we show a lack of respect for others, it stifles communication and creates barriers that are difficult to overcome.

The effectiveness of our communications is dependent upon how proficient we are in connecting with our target audience. That connection will not be complete without a mastery of other communication skills. We must devote the necessary time to ensure we not only have excellent verbal skills, but we also are complete and effective communicators.

Communication Tips

There are numerous communication points that are critical for success in any organization. Although each organization has distinct characteristics, these tips are uniformly accepted across all organizational boundaries. Taken together, they are powerful.

❖ **Communicate Success**—There is no better way to build morale and improve performance than to openly communicate the success stories of individuals or teams. It generates a sense of accomplishment, contribution, and value to the participants.

❖ **Respond to Messages Promptly**—It is important to respond to messages promptly and professionally regardless of whether received by telephone, electronically, or as formal letters. A prompt response is critical if only to acknowledge receipt and indicate that a more complete response will be forthcoming. A lack of response sends a message that the topic and the sender are unimportant.

❖ **Keep Appointments and Be Timely**—It is important to not only keep appointments but to ensure they are met on a timely basis. Either missing or being late for an appointment communicates to the other participants that either they are or the subject matter is unimportant. Additionally, it implies that their time is not valuable.

> ## Unfaithfulness in the keeping of an appointment is an act of clear dishonesty. You may as well borrow a person's money as his time.
>
> —Horace Mann (1796–1859),
> US secretary of education, college president, and statesman

❖ **Praise Publicly and Criticize Privately**—It is important to allow every individual to maintain dignity at all times. Public praise enhances the individual's self-esteem, self-respect, and eventual contribution. Public criticism embarrasses the individual and diminishes the integrity of the communicator.

❖ **Keep People Informed, Especially If It Is Bad News**—It is generally accepted that some news will be positive while other news will be negative. However, it is never acceptable to avoid communicating. Information must be shared regardless of how negative or severe and despite the implications.

❖ **Avoid Controversial Subjects**—It is always better and surely more pragmatic to avoid discussion in the workplace of controversial issues such as religion, politics, and other social issues. Most individuals have strong passions and often uniquely different opinions on these subjects. Remember, when discussing controversial issues, there are no winners. Since resolution is impossible, controversy is assured, and alienation is inevitable, avoid the discussion.

If the subject is controversial, please discuss it elsewhere.

—Alfred A. Montapert, US motivational author

❖ **Criticize the Action, Not the Individual**—It is often necessary to criticize the actions of an individual. Remember, the focus of the criticism should always be on the activity and not the employee.

❖ **Practice Effective Communication Techniques**—Recognize that practicing effective communication techniques, such as those listed below, is also quite necessary:

- **Eye Contact**—During conversation, maintain eye contact with the communication partner. Eye contact is accepted as anywhere in the nose-eye triangle.

- **Body Space**—Recognize that during personal contact you should always allow a minimum of eighteen to twenty inches of personal space around the entire body of the communication partner.

- **Handshake**—During a handshake, always maintain eye contact and offer a firm grip. It is an effective means to begin a dialogue.

❖ **Handle Employees as Individuals, Not as a Group**—Although employees may perform as a team, the team is made up of individuals with different interests, motivations, skills, and needs. Results are better achieved by recognizing and motivating the individuals within the team.

❖ **Speak in a Professional Manner**—There are times and places for releasing our complete arsenal of different expressions, actions, and theatrics. However, the professional organizational environment is not that place. Maintaining professionalism at all times, regardless of the circumstances, is essential.

❖ **Speak in a Principled Way**—Speech reflects who we are, our professionalism, and our integrity.

❖ **Adjust Message to Audience**—Recognize that different audiences require different messages, even though the messages may be on the same subject. The message is often different based on the action required. Know your audience and adjust both the message and the means of delivery to ensure effectiveness.

❖ **Be Forceful and Maintain Dignity**—Often, circumstances dictate a forceful response to individuals or actions. However, dignity must be maintained at all times to ensure the message is not overshadowed by the actions displayed.

❖ **Group Debates**—Avoid attacks against the person. Always argue issues and avoid injecting personal indictments. Allow room for the other party to escape and save face in the process.

A Controversial Issue

Some years ago, a seasoned manager was particularly concerned about school busing, which was a highly visible and, at the time, much-debated social issue. As a result of his strong beliefs and impulsive reaction, he chose the democratic process and wrote his congressman expressing his thoughts on the issue. This manager committed a major error by sharing the letter with the entire staff and encouraging them to write their congressman using his letter as an example. Although the manager had strong personal convictions and followed the democratic process, this controversial issue should not have been introduced in the workplace. The letter caused much consternation within the group and divided it into two separate camps: those supportive of his position and those who opposed. The division in the group ran along racial and ethnic lines, which further inflamed the controversy. The manager lost his effectiveness and the respect of the staff for his communication blunder. He was eventually demoted in the organization.

Lesson on Controversial Issues

There will always be political, religious, social, or environmental issues in which people have very strong personal convictions. Avoid introducing them into the work environment. These issues will create conflict, never be resolved in the work environment, negatively impact employee performance, and close the lines of communication.

There are many facets of effective communication that we often fail to recognize. Whales appear to have perfected this skill in their environment. They practice many verbal, listening, and nonverbal skills that are essential for effective communication in their environment. We should learn from their experience that focusing on verbal skills alone will not ensure effective communication. We must be as diligent as whales and employ communication skills that are relevant to our environment if we are to be effective communicators. Practicing the skills and observing the identified tips will improve communication in our organizational environment.

In silence man can most readily preserve his integrity.

—Meister Eckhart (1260–1328), German Christian mystic

Chapter Twelve

Personal Integrity and Dogs

All men, by natural intuition, feel and know common right and wrong.

—Aristotle (384–322 BC), Greek philosopher

PRINCIPLE TWELVE
Develop a Personal Code of Ethics That Includes Honesty,
Fairness, and Strong Moral Values.

Dogs: Is it Integrity or Compassion?

It has been said that dogs are a man's best friend because of the qualities they display:

- **Emotions**—They are honest about how they feel. They openly display joy, disappointment, and other emotions.

- **Love**—They love, return love freely, and openly display their affection.

- **Compassion**—They have been observed helping other animals or humans in despair.

- **Loyalty**—They remain loyal during prosperity, poverty, health, sickness, and other conditions.

- **Remorse**—They display shame or guilt for acts that are unacceptable.

- **Dignity**—They disassociate themselves from dogs that do not live up to their standards.

In spite of their tremendous qualities, it cannot be substantiated that dogs have consciousness or the free will to decide between right and wrong. For this reason, some argue that dogs do not have integrity. However, they show many of the qualities that are observed in human integrity.

Lesson Inspired by Nature

It does not matter what it is called, dogs display ethical qualities and other significant attributes. If you embrace many of these same qualities, you will have made tremendous strides toward ensuring the integrity needed for success in your career.

Strong Moral Values

In an organizational environment, as well as in our personal lives, there is nothing quite as valuable as personal integrity. Our personal integrity is rooted in the following:

- It is the foundation on which trust is developed, respect is gained, and confidence is built.

- It is an individual's moral principle, personal philosophy, or core belief as it relates to right and wrong.

- It is the basis for who we are, and it determines how others perceive us.

- It manifests itself in the actions we take and incorporates our honesty, incorruptibility, and soundness in judgment.

- It is the moral responsibility we accept to do what is fair and honest in all activities.

It is imperative that we maintain strong ethical behavior and personal integrity at all cost. Even though building character takes considerable time, it can be lost in an instant and with little or no effort. Loss of personal integrity or ethics can single-handedly prevent the reaching of our personal goals and also raise legal issues.

An Honesty Issue

Most individuals are continuously faced with circumstances where their honesty must be invoked to avoid being involved with unethical situations. A personal encounter that left me extremely uneasy occurred at a time I held a senior position in a subsidiary organization. The subsidiary had been identified for divestment because of its lack of strategic fit; the subsidiary business was not consistent with the organization's mission. We announced the decision to all employees and proceeded with the necessary preparation to solicit and accept offers for the sale. However, after an extended period of receiving and reviewing many unacceptable offers, we made a very positive announcement to all employees. We announced that the organization would discontinue its effort to divest and would remain a part of the parent organization for the foreseeable future. Obviously, the removal of this uncertainty was well received by employees. Several weeks later, a confidentiality agreement was thrust in front of me to sign, requesting my continued effort to support the sale. However, this time the effort was to be in confidence. Another unsolicited potential buyer had emerged with a more substantial offer. The rationale for the confidentiality was a reluctance to put employees back on the emotional rollercoaster. While I clearly understood the rationale and shared the concern for employees, I had considerable angst with this request. Over the years, I had developed a level of trust with the employees, had given them my word, and I personally made the announcement that all sales efforts had ended. I was being asked to work confidentially on a project that was in direct conflict with all of my statements. After considerable thought, it was impossible for me to sign the agreement, in good conscience, and I notified the subsidiary's president of my decision. Remember the tremendous loyalty noted in dogs? Perhaps this was a bit of human loyalty. Of course, I was willing to support the sale but not in a clandestine manner.

Although he indicated that he understood, he also said he thought it was the wrong decision. At the time, I was not sure of the impact or the potential consequence this would have on my career. Regardless of the implications, I was prepared to accept the consequences. Fortunately, shortly thereafter, the decision was made to notify all employees. I do not know whether my decision had an impact on the outcome. I do believe it was the ethical approach to a very delicate situation.

Lesson: An Ethical Decision

There will be times in your career when you will be confronted with a decision on an ethics, integrity, or honesty issue. Always remember to be fair and honest in all of your actions. There are few opportunities for redemption if you take the wrong path.

Always do right. This will gratify some people and astonish the rest.

—Mark Twain (1835–1910), US author and humorist

Integrity, or strong moral values, is not a local or national issue. It is a universal philosophy. The ethics issue revolves around recognition and acceptance of the Golden Rule, the principle in which religious teachings are steeped. The following list of tenets from five major faiths demonstrates the worldwide similarities in the teaching and acceptance of the same basic principle:

- **Christianity**—Do unto others as you would have others do unto you.

- **Buddhism**—Hurt not others in ways that you yourself would find hurtful.

- **Hinduism**—The true role of life is to guard and do by the things of others as they do on their own.

- **Islam**—No one of you is a believer until he desires for his brother that which he desires for himself.

- **Judaism**—Whatever is hurtful to yourself do not to your fellow man. That is the whole of the law; the rest is merely a commentary.

The underlying principle in these five major religions is to consider others and treat them fairly. This principle is the basis of personal integrity and must be included in daily organizational activities.

A Lasting Lesson

Often, there are events or conversations that leave an indelible impression. One such conversation occurred very early in my life. I was approximately seven years old. I do not remember where we were going or the reason for the conversation. However, it was a family conversation that occurred in our old, green, 1946 Pontiac with my parents and brothers all headed to this unknown destination. I recall very vividly the statement my mother made:

"I will give my life and everything I own to defend any one of you if you are in trouble and you are right. If you get in trouble and you are wrong or it is for lying, cheating, stealing, or hurting someone, you have to get out of that mess yourself."

Those words, spoken by my mother, made a tremendous impression on me, and I went through much of my early childhood believing that I could never even tell a little white lie. As I grew older, reflected on these comments, and observed her compassionate, caring, and loving nature, I know she would have supported us even under adverse circumstances. However, it was her way of emphasizing that integrity was important and worth defending with your whole being. It was her way of saying that nothing short of strong moral character was acceptable. There is no question that these words were powerful and left a tremendous impact on me. The comments also established the standards or the level of expectations that she had for each of us. Conversations such as this laid the foundation on which my strong belief in personal integrity, fairness, and honesty was developed.

Lesson on Personal Integrity

Your commitment to strong moral character and personal integrity must be evident and unyielding. It is unimportant when, where, or how your integrity was developed. The point to remember is that maintaining your personal integrity is essential for success in your personal life and in your professional career.

The dedication to honesty and fairness must always be maintained since there are many societal mores or organizational pressures that provide opportunities for diversion. The news is filled with stories of unsavory deeds that question the moral integrity of individuals and organizations. Deeds such as insider trading, price fixing, neglecting product safety, falsifying information, misleading shareholders, withholding critical information, lying, stealing, cheating, and many other dishonest actions have become extremely commonplace in the news. The frequency of these actions and the lack of remorse demonstrated by many of the accused clearly reflect a decline of personal integrity in our society. Just think, even dogs show remorse for many of their unsavory actions. In spite of the apparent decline in integrity, it is crucial to keep ourselves above the fray and steadfastly hold on to high standards of integrity regardless of the values others attempt to impose on us.

Hold yourself responsible for a higher standard than anybody else expects of you. Never excuse yourself.

—Henry Ward Beecher (1813–1887), US religious leader

Perhaps one of the most debated issues in today's organizations is that of ethics. Much of this debate is around the organization's responsibility resulting from the indiscretion of a few. This debate has gained much attention primarily because of the alleged misconduct by key members of management teams from Fortune 500 companies. These disclosures have intensified the belief by many in the general public that management was dishonest or, at the very least, less than forthcoming with pertinent information. Perhaps we should take a lesson from dogs and be honest in all of our actions. I will not attempt to pass judgment on the guilt or innocence of the companies or the management teams involved; however, the actions have cast a shadow over those organizations and public companies in general. In effect, these alleged acts have left many questioning the integrity of all organizations, not just those making the news. This negative exposure has affected not only the organizations, but it has also impacted their customers, shareholders, employees, and the families of many. What a huge price to pay for the indiscretions of a few.

You cannot do wrong without suffering wrong.

—Ralph Waldo Emerson (1803–1882), US essayist, poet, and philosopher

There have been a variety of organizational responses to the apparent integrity dilemma. The actions have often had significant impact on the behaviors and the responsibilities of employees, management, and boards of directors. For years, many organizations have required annual integrity questionnaires from most of the management and from employees with highly visible external contacts. The questionnaires often sought answers to questions that would highlight actions that were not in compliance with the organization's policies. Organizations have recently implemented, revised, reemphasized, or expanded their questionnaires. They have expanded their employee policies to document expectations, remind employees of the ethical parameters, and introduce new employees to company policies. However, these actions are just guidelines with the intended purpose of establishing parameters for employees. Yet, guidelines cannot identify all potential ethical conflicts. These guidelines are sometimes intended to protect the organizations should it be faced with unethical behaviors by some of its employees. Regardless of the rationale, there has been a rapid response by organizations to the alleged unethical behavior exposed in some large organizations. However, many of the alleged unethical activities disclosed were willful and beyond the scope of ethical questionnaires. In spite of a concerted effort by many organizations to minimize unethical behaviors, integrity is a personal issue that must be addressed individually. The best that the organization can do is to advise employees of the severe consequences if they become involved with unethical activities.

> ## Unfortunately, governments cannot legislate decency or integrity or goodness. Each individual must develop the power within himself.
>
> —Alfred A. Montapert, US motivational author

The significant response to the ethical quagmire has been swift and far reaching. Many institutions of higher learning have responded by adding additional ethics courses to their curricula in an attempt to teach ethics. In many schools, completing ethics courses is now a requirement for graduation, and some have added majors in ethics-related disciplines.

The rationale for this response is to demonstrate relevance, commitment, and evidence that graduates are well prepared and have been exposed to relevant issues. While one can question the long-term effectiveness of teaching ethics, it is, nevertheless, the academic response to the debate.

Honesty is the first chapter of the book of wisdom.

—Thomas Jefferson (1743–1826), US president

Although much has been written about ethics and relevant courses have been included in university curricula, I am not convinced that integrity can be taught in an academic environment. Personal integrity is who we are, and it manifests itself in the actions we take on specific issues. Yes, we can and should be informed of the necessity for ethical behavior; we can better understand company policies, review cases where others failed to practice ethical standards, and understand the importance of ethical behaviors in organizations. However, this exposure will not develop integrity. It can only reinforce what has been developed over the years. Since this academic exposure will not identify all unethical encounters, there must be something internal in addition to what is taught. We must have an innate quality, a yearning to do what is right, a sense of right and wrong, and strength not to be shaken from these beliefs.

In most careers, there will be incidents where the easy way would be to follow the majority and remain silent on issues that are truly unethical. Remaining quiet when confronted with integrity issues would definitely avoid confrontation. However, ignoring a wrong will not make us less culpable. We should be as steadfast in maintaining our personal integrity as dogs are in maintaining their loyalty. We must maintain an established, strong set of values, avoid deviating from them, and not allow ourselves to be influenced by the momentum or by others.

We should know what our convictions are, and
stand for them. Upon one's own philosophy,
conscious or unconscious depends one's ultimate
interpretation of facts. Therefore, it is wise to be as
clear as possible about one's subjective principles.
As the man is, so will be his ultimate truth.

—Carl Jung (1875–1961), Swiss psychiatrist

There is no question that personal integrity is one of the most important qualities needed to attain success in any organization. Because of the myriad of possibilities and the lack of a roadmap that clearly identifies all potential ethical issues, it is our personal code of ethics or our integrity that must guide us. The defining factor in determining whether we succeed or fail when faced with this dilemma is the criteria used to ensure we are always following the ethical path. In every decision, there are a number of personal questions to continuously ask ourselves to avoid misdeeds that adversely affect us, the organization, employees, customers, or shareholders. Here are some typical questions:

- Am I willingly misleading others? If the answer is yes, there is an integrity issue to address.

- Does the action remain within all legal boundaries? If not, there is a legal-compliance issue.

- Is the action designed solely for personal gain? If yes, what are the implications for others? Is there a legal-compliance issue in question?

- Is the information being presented in an objective manner, or would others have been misinformed if we had not used editorial nuances?

- Will the action be fair, even though it might not be popular? There are many tough decisions that must be made. As long as they are fair and equitable, they most likely will pass the integrity test.

- Am I being honest with myself and others and representing the information as best I can?

- Would I expect others to treat me in the same way? The basic premise here is to treat others as we want to be treated.

- Will I be able to walk by the mirror and like the person looking back? Will there be guilt remaining after the decision is rendered? Will the decision require me to live a lie afterward?

- Will I be able to openly discuss the issue later, or must it remain confidential because of potential moral outrage?

- Is the action being taken based upon a thorough and objective review? Am I making the best and most objective decision possible based on the information available? Needless to say, certain decisions often appear unfair once additional information becomes available. However, actions taken without this knowledge would be classified as mistakes in judgment if the intent was not to defraud or mislead. These mistakes are errors of omission rather than an attempt to mislead.

Even when all of the questions have been asked, answered appropriately, and the decisions made, there will be occasions when the sincerity or integrity of the decision is questioned by others. This second guessing cannot be eliminated. However, the essential point is as long as we have addressed the issue with utmost integrity, we can be confident that we have followed the ethical path.

The context in which we use integrity in this chapter is from a moral or ethical perspective. This perspective is demonstrated, accepted, and practiced as the basic principle by most of the major religions of the world. Many of the characteristics that define integrity are also reflected in dogs. That is why we refer to them as loyal. The major difference is that dogs do not have the free will to decide between right and wrong. In spite of this, they demonstrate many honorable characteristics. Even though integrity is a major tenet that is universally accepted, practiced in every environment, and taught in most universities, the incidents of reported failures are increasing significantly. We must ensure that we maintain our integrity to reverse this trend, to accomplish our goals, and to ensure our success.

Rather fail with honor than succeed by fraud.

—Sophocles (496–406 BC), Greek writer, philosopher, and playwright

Chapter Thirteen

Leadership and
Alpha Wolves

Real leaders are ordinary people with extraordinary
determination.

—Author unknown

PRINCIPLE THIRTEEN
Focus on Leadership Qualities and Employ the Style
That Fits Your Persona.

Leadership Exhibited by Alpha Wolves

We often perceive wolves as pack-dwelling, aggressive creatures with few, if any, redeeming qualities. Instead, they are some of the more highly evolved land mammals in North America. They exhibit a much-disciplined leadership hierarchy. Many of the characteristics necessary for effective leadership are evident in the leader. The wolf pack often takes on the demeanor or personality of the leader, and packs have been observed as being

- Relaxed and easygoing;
- Very hierarchical with an upper echelon;
- Assertive and aggressive;
- Extremely confrontational.

Regardless of the leadership style, the wolf pack's effectiveness is dependent upon allegiances, obedience, conformity, altruism, and cooperation. Their dependencies are affected by limited personal freedoms balanced by survival through unity. Since they hunt prey significantly larger than they are, their strength comes from the effectiveness of the leader and the pack's ability to operate as a team.

Lesson Inspired by Nature

Develop leadership qualities and follow the style that you are comfortable with, fits your demeanor, and is respected by others. The style, along with a consistent approach, will significantly improve your effectiveness.

Leadership is earned . . . not proclaimed.

—Charles "Tremendous" Johnson

The Style That Fits

Although leadership is a skill that is necessary for our personal lives as well as organizational success, it is often mistakenly associated more with position than any other factor. *Webster's New World Dictionary* defines a leader as "the guiding head" and identifies terms often used in relation to leadership: "authority," "control," "administration," "effectiveness," "superiority," "supremacy," and "energy." Although these terms are associated with leadership, they are of limited value in helping us develop leadership skills. They do not address the leadership qualities nor do they identify the attributes necessary to be effective as a leader. In this context, the focus will be on the qualities needed to develop leadership skills.

The very essence of all power to influence lies in getting the other person to participate. The mind that can do that has a powerful leverage on his human world.

—Harold A. Overstreet

In *Developing the Leader within You*, John Maxwell states that "leadership is influence" or "the ability to obtain followers." The ability to exert influence and obtain followers is essential to continue advancing in most organizations. One of the significant leadership qualities of alpha wolves is the significant influence they exert over the wolf pack. Influence encourages others to believe in the leader and to get the tasks accomplished. This belief results in greater commitment, motivation, willingness, and energy by the participants.

Since leadership is influence, our goal must be to determine how to develop influence. There is no magic leadership formula since effective leaders have many unique styles. Personal qualities will influence the approach we take toward leadership and the style we finally develop. However, there are three basic skill categories that we must master before we can attain the necessary influence. The categories are:

- **Strong Interpersonal Skills**—The ability to gain respect, relate, and connect with others;

- **Recognizable Competence**—The basic knowledge and awareness of the organization's issues;

- **Effective Communication Skills**—The ability to verbalize, listen, and master nonverbal cues.

These are skills that are easily recognizable and are the basis upon which we gain influence. Focusing on developing these skills is essential if we are to attain the level of influence and the leadership we are seeking.

I suppose leadership at one time meant muscles; but today it means getting along with people.

—Indira Gandhi (1917–1984), Indian prime minister

Often, the identified leader can demand the completion of a task and the demand is dutifully followed by others. People comply because the person making the demand is in a higher position in the organization. However, this is coercion, and it does not necessarily indicate true leadership. Similarly, there are individuals who can guide a well-defined task to a successful conclusion. This is more of a management process than a leadership skill. While leadership often entails management and sometimes coercion, it also requires vision. It requires the ability to recognize a problem, plan the actionable solution, influence others, and guide the task to a successful conclusion.

The manager manages, the leader leads.

—Tony Boswell, attorney and entrepreneur

The manager administers, the leader innovates. The manager maintains, the leader develops. The manager relies on systems, the leader relies on people. The manager counts on controls, the leader counts on trust. The manager does things right, the leader does the right thing.

—Fortune Magazine

The leadership position in life is often the basis for measuring personal accomplishments or organizational success. In spite of the significance attributed to the position, there is no quick or easy ladder since leadership must be earned. It is through continuously displaying ordinary character traits such as trust, sincerity, honesty, and integrity that we earn the respect and gain influence over others. It is also earned through performance, relationship building, sound decision making, effective communication, competence, and empathy for others. It is through the utilization of these qualities and eventual recognition by others that confidence is built and leadership earned.

Leadership Qualities Described

During a discussion with a group of undergraduate students, I was asked to identify the five leadership qualities that employees would use to describe me. While it is often difficult to objectively critique oneself, I described the dominant qualities as follows:

- **People Skills**—Most would say that I am an effective listener, am fair, and have a genuine concern for team members. I am responsive to the needs of the team as well as the organization.

- **Competent**—Most would acknowledge that I have devoted the time and effort to be competent in my field yet am wise enough to listen to reason.

- **Strong Character**—Employees would say that they are confident that I am trustworthy, have strong ethical standards, and will not ask them to sacrifice their integrity. I would not ask them to do anything I would not do.

- **Focused**—Employees would acknowledge that my strengths are in identifying the tasks, planning the actions, and devoting the manpower toward accomplishing the objectives.

- **Adaptable**—Because the environment, technology, and people are ever-changing, they would say I have demonstrated the willingness and ability to recognize and adjust to these changes for the benefit of the team.

I continued the response by saying that I believe that my role as a leader is to surround myself with capable individuals with different personalities, skills, thoughts, talents, and ideas. Once that is done, my leadership role is to conduct the orchestra of differences in perfect harmony.

Lesson: Know Your Leadership Qualities

Understand the dominant leadership qualities that are your strengths. Develop the skills that are consistent with your personality to ensure your readiness when opportunities are available.

Since most organizations accomplish their objectives by utilizing teams, and all teams require leadership, it necessarily follows that leadership is a prerequisite to long-term organizational success. There is no substitute or a way to avoid the necessity for strong leadership skills. Because of its significance, early development and practice of these skills will definitely aid preparation for the task. It is incumbent on each of us to be ready to accept the leadership challenge if our goal involves organizational success.

Failed Leadership

A major role of my team was to provide administrative support to the organization. Because of this role, we often received feedback from managers, employees, and service providers on the quality of the service. While feedback was encouraged, it was most often provided in a demanding, albeit professional, manner. On this one occasion, a colleague requested a meeting with me and my human resource management team to discuss a project we were implementing jointly. After the polite greetings, he began to berate my managers unmercifully as we all sat in shock. Clearly, it was not his role or responsibility to discipline my team of managers. I should have made the decision to stop the meeting, ask my managers to excuse themselves, and discuss the issues with my colleague privately. Instead of taking the leadership role and standing up for my team, I left them unprotected. I allowed the berating to continue for a period of time. Until today, I cannot explain my inaction nor was I able to rationalize it to my management team. The best I could do was to apologize for my failure and move forward.

Lesson: Judgemental Errors

In spite of your best effort, you will have errors in judgment. Acknowledge your errors, which everyone is already well aware of, and use the experiences as opportunities for growth rather than reasons for failure.

Much has been written about the different styles of leadership. These styles include dictatorial, consultative, consensus, discussion, and many others. Remember the different leadership styles of alpha wolves? Categorization of leadership styles is extremely broad and oversimplified. Effective leaders can be identified in all of these categories and with a variety of other individual styles. There are no prototypes. Although most leaders have many similar characteristics, they are manifested in different ways. Because of this, it is important for us to develop and maintain a leadership style that is consistent with our personalities, our general makeup, or just who we are as individuals. Avoid attempting to develop a style that will fit a specific category. Recognize and build on personal skills. They are the basis for building our own assuredness, maintaining confidence, and ensuring consistency in our decision making. It is often ineffective to imitate another's leadership style since it leads to inconsistencies in decision making. Be genuine, maintain confidence, develop personal skills, display integrity, and emulate others only when consistent with our style. These are all keys to developing strong leadership skills.

Strong Leaders I've Known

We often associate leadership with position and expect the leader to be outgoing, effervescent, and domineering. Over the years, I have been associated with many effective leaders. Even though their styles were different, just as we noted the different leadership styles of alpha wolves, their effectiveness was not diminished. Below are a few notable characteristics of some of these leaders:

❖ **Demanding**—This leader was a brilliant, quietly demanding individual; however, he was just as demanding of himself. His reputation was well known in the organization, but that did not prevent employees from seeking employment under his direct leadership. He displayed many leadership characteristics, and above all, he was fair and respected the staff. He later became chief executive of a major international organization.

❖ **Respected**—There are leaders who gain their influence because of the respect that they gain over a period of time. The respect can result from exemplary performance, character, knowledge, style, prior accomplishment, or other noteworthy characteristics. Respected leaders become effective over time as others observe and associate with the individual. My most memorable respected leader eventually served as chief executive of a major federal agency.

❖ **Moral**—Influence is often gained from the moral strength evident in the individual. Although moral strength is a major factor in the leadership of many religious leaders, others gain their strength from these actions. One notable leader I've known is extremely reserved. Nevertheless, his influence is widespread. His leadership is evident in his moral character, oratorical skills, community involvement, political influence, and national leadership.

❖ **Principled**—Effectiveness of leaders is often earned by the manner in which they treat others. It is well known and accepted that the leader will be supportive of the team and will not tolerate a lack of integrity on anyone's part. Employees' belief in their leader is fostered by a style that provides comfort, motivates others, improves teamwork, and promotes loyalty. Leaders are often very active participants in team activities. My most memorable principled leader later became chief executive of a major national organization.

All of these leaders were extremely effective, but their styles were remarkably different. The common thread was that they all displayed many similar leadership skills.

Lesson on Leadership Skills

Your effectiveness as a leader will not be determined solely by your style. The most important point is to develop leadership skills and use those skills in a style that fits with your personality.

To lead the people, walk behind them.

—Lao Tzu (sixth century BC), Chinese philosopher

While effective leaders all have different styles, they share many similar, identifiable qualities. However, the leaders are unique in that they utilize these qualities differently. To be effective leaders, we must develop ourselves as (1) communicators, (2) listeners, (3) visionaries, (4) motivators, (5) team players, (6) mountain viewers, and (7) self-starters who are (8) competent, (9) focused, (10) empathetic, (11) responsible, (12) results oriented, (13) strong in character, (14) positive, (15) adaptable/flexible, and (16) committed.

❖ **Communicators**—Leaders must be able to effectively verbalize, with passion, the ideas, thoughts, and directions in a clear and concise manner. It must also be in a language that can be understood by all. In addition to excellent verbalization skills, they must show consistent nonverbal cues and be able to communicate effectively through presentations and written skills.

❖ **Listeners**—Leaders must be able to connect with others. This connection involves giving attention to and being able to hear others' thoughts, ideas, and opinions. The leader must then utilize that input in a meaningful manner. They must be able to motivate others by creating a sense of involvement and contribution.

❖ **Visionaries**—Leaders must have foresight or be able to anticipate and plan for future requirements. They must also be able to translate the vision into employable, long-range strategies, to influence others, and to guide the project to completion.

❖ **Motivators**—Leaders must be able to inspire others, generate excitement, and create the desire and willingness to be an active and involved participant. The resulting output will be greater if employees are inspired and involved. Recognize that there must be a sense of teaching and learning throughout the process.

❖ **Team Players**—Leaders must be fair, equitable, and recognized as keeping the best interest of the team as the primary goal at all times. They must have a strong commitment to relationship building and be willing to acknowledge and share team successes. They cannot be seen as self-centered. They must be willing to accept that there is no "I" in "team."

❖ **Mountain Viewers**—Leaders must be able to gain a broad overview of projects, identify issues, and work toward accomplishing the organization's goals. They must be able to see the big picture clearly and keep the goals in perspective.

❖ **Self-Starters**—Leaders must be able to identify issues, understand the significance, plan employable actions, maintain self-discipline, and demonstrate an infectious drive toward goal accomplishment. They do not wait to be instructed on the appropriate action. Instead, they initiate the action.

❖ **Competent**—Leaders must be competent, have problem-solving ability, and be extremely strong technically. However, being competent does not imply that they must be the most knowledgeable person in the group. Instead, they must be able to decipher information, determine its relevance, and utilize all of the available talent of the team.

> ## A leader has the vision and conviction that a dream can be achieved. He inspires the power and energy to get it done.
>
> —Ralph Lauren, US fashion designer

❖ **Focused**—Leaders must not get bogged down in insignificant details or in minutiae. They must have a clear idea of organizational direction, identify key issues, and focus only on areas that will deliver results.

❖ **Empathetic**—Leaders must have genuine concern for the well-being of others within the organization and display a genuine concern in a manner that will engender trust and loyalty. Employees are more responsive if they believe the leader respects them as individuals instead of treating them as objects.

❖ **Responsible**—Leaders must be dependable, accountable for the achievement, and answerable for potential failures of the team. They must be able to confront reality and demonstrate a level of acceptance for uncertainty in times of disappointments.

❖ **Results Oriented**—Leaders must look to the future, plan, organize, effectively monitor progress, assure added value, achieve success, and focus on the attainment of goals. Emphasis must be directed toward making sure the team accomplishes its objectives.

> **Personality can open doors, but only character can keep them open.**
>
> —Elmer G. Letterman

❖ **Strong in Character**—Leaders must have credibility, strong ethical values, moral strength, and even temperament while maintaining a sense of humility.

❖ **Positive**—Leaders must reflect a positive, confident attitude toward the organizational goals and objectives. Others are impacted, either negatively or positively, by the attitude or the passion of the leader.

❖ **Adaptable/Flexible**—Leaders must be adaptable, flexible, and able to adjust strategies to accomplish the overall objective. Since the environment is constantly evolving, projects are continuously developing, and other circumstances are changing, it is essential to maintain awareness and determine the potential project impact.

❖ **Committed**—Leaders must demonstrate a level of responsibility that is beyond reproach. Their commitment to the project, the team, and the organization must be infectious and transferable to the entire team.

205

Organizational Leadership Skills

Over the years, I have been actively involved with and observed effective leaders in large international organizations, large government entities, and community-based organizations. While leadership skills were similar in the different organizations, the manner in which they were practiced differed substantially.

❖ **Private Organizations**—Leaders in private organizations followed a more formal process in that issues were identified, input sought from others, and a final decision made after considering the input. Once the decision was made, the expectation was that the organization would unite behind the decision and commit to pursuing it to a logical conclusion. Objectivity was maintained through more formal research of the issues and input from others. The effectiveness, however, was dependent upon the leader's ability to exercise influence and motivate others to accomplish the objectives. There was little overt external opposition in the implementation phase.

❖ **Government Entities**—Leaders in government organizations followed a process that involves issues identification and input from others, followed by a decision. However, there were other factors negatively affecting commitment and implementation that were absent in private organizations.

Some individuals failed to unite behind the leader or to commit to the project if they did not personally believe in the agreed solution. Because of the many political appointees, there was a belief that if they delayed implementation long enough the politically appointed leader would be gone. Their solution could again be presented for consideration.

There was an overarching concern about the political implications or the potential negative public perception of some decisions. As a result, decisions were sometimes made to avoid the potential negative perception although they may not have been the logical economic solution.

Although these factors and political considerations made leadership more challenging in the public sector, they did not diminish the need for similar leadership qualities as those noted in private organizations.

❖ **Community-Based Organizations**—Because organizations are much smaller, leaders in community-based organizations operate in a significantly less formalized structure. The informal approach can be attributed to smaller staffs, smaller areas of responsibility, and significantly less funding. The objective is to invest the available dollars in accomplishing the organization's mission rather than in staff support. Because of these factors, leaders are less specialized. They are more directly involved in daily activities, which require more knowledge and experience in the organization's objectives and goals. The advantage is that the leader is afforded the opportunity to experience all facets of the operations. People skills, influence, and believability are critical attributes to the community-based organization's leaders.

Regardless of whether our organizational interest is private, public, or community-based, the leadership skills required are uniformly applicable, even though the utilization differs substantially.

Lesson on Leadership Qualities

Focus on developing strong leadership qualities rather than a specific style. The qualities are universally applicable in any organization while styles are not necessarily transferable. Effective personal leadership skills will prepare you to pursue your long-term goals.

Concentrating only on developing an effective leadership style can be self-defeating. Instead, we should direct our effort toward developing the skills necessary for effective leadership, incorporating those skills into our individual persona, and focusing total effort on our personal strengths. This is the approach practiced successfully by alpha wolves in their environment. We noted that they have individual personalities and the wolf pack's style adapts to the demeanor of the leader. The style does not impact the effectiveness since alpha wolves develop and maintain leadership skills. Regardless of the environment, if we develop the necessary qualities, we will gain the influence necessary for leadership. It is through a consistent approach and demonstrating these qualities that we become effective and accomplish our long term goals.

As for the best leader, the people do not notice their existence. The next best, the people know and praise. The next, the people fear, and the next, the people hate. When the best leaders' work is done, the people say, we did it ourselves.

—Lao Tzu (sixth century BC), Chinese philosopher

Chapter Fourteen

Balance and Prairie Dogs

Live your life each day as you would climb a mountain. An occasional glance toward the summit keeps the goal in mind, but many beautiful scenes are to be observed from each new vantage point. Climb slowly, steadily, enjoying each passing moment; and the view from the summit will serve as a fitting climax for the journey.

—Harold V. Metchert

PRINCIPLE FOURTEEN
Maintain Balance to Ensure a Healthy Quality of Life.

The Balance of Prairie Dogs

Prairie dogs are social rodents that live in well-organized towns consisting of a multitude of mounds and earthen fortifications covering a wide area. In warmer months, they spend considerable time feeding and building their mounds and burrows that include side tunnels, rooms, and escape routes. These mounds are flood resistant, and they maintain a lifestyle balanced by the following:

- Extended social groups and family territories

- A social order or hierarchy

- Awareness of the presence or activities of neighbors

- A sense of playfulness, even into adulthood

- Friendship by much kissing and grooming of one another

- A caring attitude by making any burrow available for escape in case of danger

Prairie dogs also maintain time for repose. During winter months many species retreat to their burrows to hibernate for the winter.

Lesson Inspired by Nature

Maintain balance in your life, and include time for work, fun, family, friends, and repose. By doing so, you experience some happiness and contentment as you pursue your goal.

> Just as a cautious businessman avoids investing all his capital in one concern, so wisdom would probably admonish us also not to anticipate all our happiness from one quarter alone.

—Sigmund Freud (1856–1939), Austrian psychiatrist

Quality of Life

Reaching career goals and advancing in organizations are important, rate extremely highly, and are significant accomplishments. However, they should represent only a segment of our total life. Always keep career goals in perspective, and seek to maintain a well-balanced and healthy quality of life. Yes, we should always ensure adequate preparation, employ a strong work ethic, and give 100% effort in the pursuit of goals. Yet, we should incorporate other activities into our lives to avoid making career advancement our sole activity or focus.

Ensure priorities are in order and maintain a healthy balance of physical, social, mental, and spiritual activities. It is also important to include time for family, friends, social activities, extracurricular activities, exercise, travel, and rest in our lives. Including these activities will enable us to perform more effectively, add purpose and enjoyment to life, and remove the possibility of becoming one dimensional. There are many workaholics who advance to significantly high levels in organizations. However, from my observation, many lack the balance necessary for a healthy and happy quality of life. These workaholics eventually burn out or lose their position and, because of the lack of balance, are left disillusioned. They have no other means of identity. Additionally, all of us require some diversions or outlets from the tremendous stress that is often present in positions within an organizational environment.

> If a man insisted on being serious and never allowed himself a bit of fun and relaxation, he would go mad or become unstable without knowing it.
>
> —Herodotus (484–430 BC), Greek writer and historian

Recognize that life must have much more meaning than just organizational performance. Our careers, while important, should not define who we are nor should they become our sole identity. Instead we should (1) maintain quality family relationships, (2) maintain healthy lifestyles, (3) include fun activities, (4) nurture belief systems, (5) connect with others through community activities, and (6) keep success in perspective.

❖ **Maintain Quality Family Relationships**—Make sure that your routine includes enjoying family, being a friend, and balancing life. Because of the need for continuous support, it is the family relationship that provides the genuineness and lasting support since it is based on personal caring and total well-being. The family relationship provides the strong support and understanding necessary when we are faced with adversity or stress, which is inevitable in our lives. It provides grounding, which is essential for growth. Positions may change and career advancement may stagnate, but families are forever. Like prairie dogs, we must nourish our relationships, for they provide support when needed.

Friends

As our children were growing up, we often initiated Christmas projects to deemphasize the holiday's commercial focus. One particular holiday, we decided to distribute sandwiches, fruit, and cookies to sixty homeless people around the city. While we prepared the individual packages for delivery later that night, we discussed the importance of being concerned about the welfare of others. Later that frigid Christmas Eve, we stopped to give a package to an disheveled elderly gentleman. He appeared extremely appreciative, but as he accepted the package, he commented, "Don't forget my friend. He is located on the corner of 12th Street and Superior Avenue." He followed that by saying, "He always looks out for me." Those comments reverberated in my thoughts for some time. Even under these adverse conditions, this disheveled homeless man was still concerned about someone else.

Lesson on Personal Anchors

Don't forget your family and friends. Even though there will be occasions when your path seems unclear, remember, they are the anchors that will provide you with needed support.

Everyone only goes around the track once in life, and if you don't enjoy that trip, it's pretty pathetic.

—Gary Rogers

❖ **Maintain Healthy Lifestyles**—It is important to maintain healthy lifestyles while pursuing our career goals. In this context, healthy lifestyles include both diet and exercise. Our bodies really are our temples, and we should be diligent to ensure they are maintained at all times. I am not suggesting that we follow a strict and regimented approach. Instead, we must always remain conscious of our intake and follow an exercise program that can be maintained. A healthy lifestyle will positively impact our mental and physical health. Following a healthy lifestyle program will also enable us to improve our appearance, maintain mental awareness, stay focused, develop self-confidence, and pursue the balanced quality of life we are seeking.

❖ **Include Fun Activities**—Take the time to enjoy the journey; smell the roses as you progress toward your career goals. Remember how prairie dogs maintain social groups, a sense of playfulness, and friendships in their lives? We should be just as intent on including fun things in our lives. Travel, include extracurricular activities, and incorporate other fun activities into your life. It is through the inclusion of external activities that we experience personal growth. However, in the process, we also reduce stress, incorporate balance, improve performance, and avoid burnout.

❖ **Nurture Belief Systems**—Recognize that our health, happiness, and success results from an abundant flow of positive energy. Accept that this positive energy is a gift from a universal source. Be thankful for those things we do have and cherish them. It is from this relationship that we gain strength, endurance, patience, and peace of mind to continue the journey toward our goals.

Sunshine, songs of birds, the blue heavens, sunrise, the sea air, the field full of flowers, the magenta sunset, love, joy, peace of mind, the wonders of nature, the warm rain, the dew on the roses, the love of God, etc., are here for our enjoyment.

—Alfred A. Montapert, US motivational author

❖ **Connect with Others through Community Activities**—Include the time to share with others some of what we have been given. Even prairie dogs demonstrate this community spirit by sharing their burrows in time of need. For us, connecting involves lending our voices, giving our times, and providing support to others needing champions, assistance, or encouragement. We are as a tiny drop of water that, viewed alone, is rather insignificant. Yet, as part of the vast sea, we are extremely powerful. As a part of the universe, we cannot live in isolation. Because of this, it is important that we do our part to make this universe a more meaningful place to live and work. This includes extending a helping hand to others, providing service to mankind, and helping our organizations become better corporate citizens. By doing these things, the benefits of our effort will enable us to also enjoy happiness and success.

Cause and Effect

My brothers and I grew up in a family with parents who believed in tough love. The tough love was punctuated with comments designed to teach us values that could be used for a lifetime. Although we did not always know the reason why, understand the comments, want to hear them, or appreciate their value, they were a regular part of our daily lives. Some of the comments are listed below:

- You reap what you sow.

- You get out of life only what you put into it.

- What goes around comes around.

- Somewhere along the line you will get it back.

- If you hold your hand so tight to avoid sharing, nothing can get into the hand either.

- You got what was coming to you.

These comments, heard frequently in our home, were our parent's way of continuously impressing upon us the need for involvement and connecting with others. Inherent in the messages was that without the connection, we could never realize our potential.

Lesson: Personal Involvement

Community involvement will assist in maintaining balance in your life. In addition, you benefit personally from the involvement and experience a more meaningful, enjoyable, and fulfill life.

❖ **Keep Success in Perspective**—We must always recognize that personal success is a gift that should be enjoyed. However, success can be fleeting and vanish in an instant. Maintain humility and understand that not all of our families, friends, and coworkers will share in our joy or wish for our continued success. While we may not understand the rationale, we must accept the reality. Always remember, much of what we achieve is because of what others have given.

Martha's Connection to Others

There was one employee who left a tremendous impression on me. After one of our company's reorganizations and a significant reduction in the workforce, we selected employees to fill the new positions. One day, Martha's name appeared on my calendar for a brief appointment. She had requested the meeting but did not identify a topic for discussion. Martha, a middle-aged employee, had a historically strong performance record and had been selected for one of my key positions in the new organization. Since there was no meeting topic identified, I assumed that she wanted to better understand the expectations of the position. I mistakenly assumed that the meeting would focus primarily on her new position. After exchanging pleasantries, I began the discussion about the new position:

- Personally congratulating her on the selection.

- Discussing the importance of the appointment.

- Identifying how her talents matched the position.

- Outlining the expectations the organization had for her.

- Expressing confidence that she could fulfill all of these expectations.

In fact, I was particularly proud of the conversation's flow and believed that I had made a positive impression on her. After my comments, she politely indicated that although she was appreciative of the selection and the confidence we had in her, it was not the reason she made the appointment. She said, "Rather than accepting this position, may I give it to Francis? Because she is a single mother and needs the job much more than I do." (Francis was one of the casualties of the reduction in workforce.) My response was that although I applauded her concern and wished that I could accommodate her request, it was only fair that we maintain objectivity in the selection process. I added that if she declined the position, I would then select the next best qualified person, and it might not be Francis. She hesitated and said, "I understand and thought that you would say that." However, Martha followed that request by saying, "Well, if you can't give Francis the job, can I take some time off before starting the new job? I want to donate one of my kidneys to my daughter. She is on dialysis, has a little four-year-old daughter, and needs the kidney much more than I do to raise that child." Needless to say, I sat stunned and momentarily speechless. Even though the new position represented a significant advancement, Martha's concerns were not personal. Instead, her concerns were focused on the well-being of others. Her actions demonstrated a concern for family and friends and focused less on personal position or status. I've often thought back over this conversation and marveled at the love, the empathy, the spirit, the concern, and the balance Martha seemed to have in her life. Yes, she had a very successful career. At the same time, she kept life in perspective. She understood very clearly that while her career was important and required perseverance, commitment, and hard work, career success alone was not sufficient to sustain life.

> ## Lesson: Balance in Life
> Although careers and personal progress are important, they alone cannot sustain you. You must include other activities and relationships to maintain a successful, happy, and balanced quality of life.

We must maintain balance in our lives as we continuously seek the accomplishment of our professional goals. We noted that prairie dogs maintain balance in their environment. Their balance enhances relationships, provides for personal needs, improves safety, and enables survival of the group. We should be just as diligent in incorporating other individuals and activities in our lives. This balance will improve our performance and the quality of our lives.

> Any man is wealthy who has good health, a happy home life, a business profession in which he is interested and successful, a passion for growth, and the ambition to be of service to his fellow men.
>
> —Richard W. Sampson (1470–1554), English religious leader

Epilogue

Summary of Principles

Principle One
Know Yourself, Accept Yourself, and Be Yourself
Regardless of the Consequences.

Principle Two
Acknowledge That Adaptability Is Essential
to an Effective Transition.

Principle Three
Establish Goals to Add Direction, Purpose, Focus,
and Meaning to Life.

Principle Four
Pursue Competence, Develop Marketable Skills, Polish Image,
and Practice Professionalism.

Principle Five
Recognize That Motivated, Disciplined, Committed,
and Persistent Performance Is Essential.

Principle Six
Understand That Success or Failure Is an Attitudinal Issue.

Principle Seven
Foster Relationships to Enhance Recognition, Ensure Development, Create Opportunities, and Promote Success.

Principle Eight
Recognize That Teamwork Is Essential to Accomplish Personal, Professional, and Organizational Goals.

Principle Nine
Maintain Knowledge of Organizational Environmental Issues and Ensure Compatibility with Personal Values.

Principle Ten
Advocate When Necessary and Pause When Required.

Principle Eleven
Develop and Maintain Effective Verbal, Nonverbal, Listening, and Interaction Skills.

Principle Twelve
Develop a Personal Code of Ethics That Includes Honesty, Fairness, and Strong Moral Values.

Principle Thirteen
Focus on Leadership Qualities and Employ the Style That Fits Your Persona.

Principle Fourteen
Maintain Balance to Ensure a Healthy Quality of Life.

Bibliography

Agel, Jerome, and Walter D. Glanze. *Pearls of Wisdom: A Harvest of Quotations from All Ages*. Toronto: Harper and Row, 1987.

Bekoff, Mark. *Minding Animals: Awareness, Emotion, and Heart*. New York: Oxford University Press, 2002.

Belasco, James A. *The Ten Commandments of Success*. Beverly Hills, CA: New Millennium Press, 2000.

Benyus, Janine. *Beastly Behaviors*. Reading, MA: Addison-Wesley, 1992.

Boothman, Nicholas. *How to Connect in Business in 90 Seconds or Less*. New York: Workman, 2002.

Brem, Marion Luna. *The 7 Greatest Truths about Successful Women*. New York: Penguin Putnam, 2000.

Brooks, Donna, and Lynn Brooks. *Ten Secrets of Successful Men that Women Want to Know*. New York: McGraw Hill, 2002.

Brown, H. Jackson, Jr. *A Father's Book of Wisdom*. Nashville, TN: Rutledge Hill Press, 1988.

Cairo, Jim. *Motivation and Goal Setting: How to Set and Achieve Goals and Inspire Others*. Franklin Lakes, NJ: Career Press, 1998.

Capezio, Peter. *Winning Teams: Making Your Team Productive & Successful*. Franklin Lakes, NJ: Career Press, 1998.

Caras, Roger. *The Private Lives of Animals*. New York: McGraw Hill, 1987.

Chopra, Deepak. *The Seven Spiritual Laws of Success*. San Rafael, CA: Amber-Allen, 1993.

Clark, Caroline V. *Take a Lesson: Today's Black Achievers on How They Made It and What They Learned along the Way*. New York: John Wiley and Sons, 2001.

Conner, Richard, and Dawn Micklethwaite Peterson. *The Lives of Whales and Dolphins*. New York: Henry Holt, 1994.

Cook, John, comp. and arr. *The Rubicon Dictionary of Positive, Motivational, Life Affirming and Inspirational Quotations*. Newington, CT: Rubicon Press, 1993.

Cook, Wade B. *Wade Cook's Power Quotes*. Vol. 1. Seattle, WA: Lighthouse, 1998.

Costello, David F. *The World of the Prairie Dog*. Philadelphia: J. B. Lippincott, 1970.

Davis, Phyllis. *E2—Using the Power of Ethics and Etiquette in American Business*. New York: Entrepreneur Press, 2003.

Farb, Peter. *The Insects*. Alexandria, VA: Time Life Books, 1980.

Fitzhenry, Robert I., ed. *Barnes and Noble Book of Quotations*. New York: Barnes and Noble Books, 1987.

Forbes, B. C. *The Forbes Scrapbook of Thoughts on the Business of Life*. New York: B. C. Forbes and Sons, 1976.

Fox, Michael W. *The Soul of the Wolf*. Boston: Little, Brown, 1980.

Grossman, Ned. *How to Succeed in Life: Ideas and Principles They Don't Teach in School*. Shaker Heights, OH: Diamond, 1996.

Halliday, Tim, ed. *Animal Behavior*. Norman, OK: University of Oklahoma Press, 1994.

Hill, Napoleon. *Think and Grow Rich*. New York: Random House, 1960.

Hogan, Kevin, and Robin Stubbs. *Can't Get Through—8 Barriers to Communication*. Gretna, LA: Pelican, 2003.

Lamonte, Bob, and Robert L. Shook. *Winning the NFL Way—Leadership Lessons from Football's Top Head Coaches.* New York: Harper Collins, 2004.

Levine, Stuart R. *The Six Fundamentals of Success: The Rules for Getting It Right for Yourself and Your Organization.* Currency Books/Doubleday, 2004.

Maisel, Eric, PhD. *20 Communication Tips @ Work—A Quick and Easy Guide to Successful Business Relationships.* Novato, CA: New World Library, 2001.

Maxwell, John C. *Developing the Leader within You.* Nashville, TN: Thomas Nelson, 1993.

———*The 17 Essential Qualities of a Team Player—Becoming the Kind of Person Every Team Wants.* Nashville, TN: Nelson, 2002.

———*The 21 Indispensable Qualities of a Leader: Becoming the Person Others Will Want to Follow.* Nashville, TN: Nelson, 1999.

———*The 21 Irrefutable Laws of Leadership-Follow Them and People Will Follow You.* Nashville, TN: Nelson, 1998.

Montapert, Alfred Armand. *Inspiration and Motivation.* Englewood Cliffs, NJ: Prentice Hall, 1982.

Munro-Faure, Malcolm, and Lesley Munro-Faure. *The Success Culture: How to Build an Organization with Vision and Purpose.* London: Pitman Publishing, 1996.

Bibliography

Orsborn, Carol M. *Inner Excellence at Work—The Path to Meaning, Spirit, and Success.* New York: Amacom Books, 2000.

Robins, Harvey, and Michael Finley. *The New Why Teams Don't Work.* San Francisco: Berrett-Koehler Publishers, 2000.

Rue, Leonard Lee, III. *The World of the White Tailed Deer.* Philadelphia: J. B. Lippincott, 1962.

Sims, Ronald R., and John G. Veres III. *Keys to Employee Success in Coming Decades.* Westport, CT: Quorum Books, 1999.

Spiegel, Jerry, and Cresencio Torres. *Manager's Official Guide to Team Working.* San Diego: Pfeiffer, 1994.

Spina, Vicki. *Success 2000—Moving into the Millennium with Purpose, Power, and Prosperity.* New York: John Wiley and Sons, 1997.

Teale, Edwin Way. *The Strange Lives of Familiar Insects.* New York: Dodd, Mead and Company, 1964.

Wagner, Dorothy. *Rx Prescription for Success.* St. Claire Shores, MI: Insty Prints, 1987.

Ziglar, Zig. *Success for Dummies.* Foster City, CA: IDG Books, 1997.

Notes

Notes